IMAGES OF WAR

WAFFEN-SS ARMOUR ON THE EASTERN FRONT 1941–45

RARE PHOTOGRAPHS FROM WARTIME ARCHIVES

Ian Baxter

Pen & Sword
MILITARY

First published in Great Britain in 2021 by
PEN & SWORD MILITARY
an imprint of
Pen & Sword Books Ltd
47 Church Street
Barnsley
South Yorkshire
S70 2AS

ISBN 978-1-39909-003-2

A CIP catalogue record for this book is available from the British Library.

Typeset by Concept, Huddersfield, West Yorkshire HD4 5JL
Printed and bound in England by CPI Group (UK) Ltd, Croydon CR0 4YY

MIX
Paper from responsible sources
FSC® C013604
www.fsc.org

Pen & Sword Books Limited incorporates the imprints of Atlas, Archaeology, Aviation, Discovery, Family History, Fiction, History, Maritime, Military, Military Classics, Politics, Select, Transport, True Crime, Air World, Frontline Publishing, Leo Cooper, Remember When, Seaforth Publishing, The Praetorian Press, Wharncliffe Local History, Wharncliffe Transport, Wharncliffe True Crime and White Owl.

For a complete list of Pen & Sword titles please contact
PEN & SWORD BOOKS LIMITED
47 Church Street, Barnsley, South Yorkshire S70 2AS, England
E-mail: enquiries@pen-and-sword.co.uk
Website: www.pen-and-sword.co.uk

Contents

About the Author

Ian Baxter is a military historian who specialises in German twentieth-century military history. He has written more than sixty books including *Poland – The Eighteen Day Victory March, Panzers In North Africa, The Ardennes Offensive, The Western Campaign, The 12th SS Panzer-Division Hitlerjugend, The Waffen-SS on the Western Front, The Waffen-SS on the Eastern Front, The Red Army at Stalingrad, Elite German Forces of World War II, Armoured Warfare, German Tanks of War, Blitzkrieg, Panzer-Divisions at War, Hitler's Panzers, German Armoured Vehicles of World War Two, Last Two Years of the Waffen-SS at War, German Soldier Uniforms and Insignia, German Guns of the Third Reich, Defeat to Retreat: The Last Years of the German Army At War 1943–45, Operation Bagration – the Destruction of Army Group Centre, German Guns of the Third Reich, Rommel and the Afrika Korps, U-Boat War*, and most recently *The Sixth Army and the Road to Stalingrad*. He has written over a hundred articles including 'Last days of Hitler', 'Wolf's Lair', 'The Story of the V1 and V2 Rocket Programme', 'Secret Aircraft of World War Two', 'Rommel at Tobruk', 'Hitler's War With his Generals', 'Secret British Plans to Assassinate Hitler', 'The SS at Arnhem', 'Hitlerjugend', 'Battle of Caen 1944', 'Gebirgsjäger at War', 'Panzer Crews', 'Hitlerjugend Guerrillas', 'Last Battles in the East', 'The Battle of Berlin', and many more. He has also reviewed numerous military studies for publication, supplied thousands of photographs and important documents to various publishers and film production companies worldwide, and lectures to various schools, colleges and universities throughout the United Kingdom and the Republic of Ireland.

Introduction

This book is a unique visual account of the Waffen-SS armour on the Eastern Front which provides the reader with a wide selection of rare and unpublished photographs accompanied by in-depth captions and text. The images reveal the unfolding story of the Waffen-SS as it battled its way across Russia employing Panzers and supporting armoured vehicles as the main striking force, which scored a number of sizable victories against a foe that appeared to be on the verge of defeat. It shows these vehicles in various battles, such as the recapture of Kharkov in early 1943, the Kursk offensive and battles fought out in the Baltic States, central Russia during Operation BAGRATION, its withdrawal through Poland in 1944 and then into the Reich a few months later.

The photos portray how these formidable Waffen-SS armoured units adapted and up-gunned their vehicles to face the ever-increasing enemy threat. It shows how these armoured crews with their Pz.Kpfw.I, II, III, IV, Panther, Tiger, King Tiger, assault and self-propelled guns used offensive tactics during defensive battles and how units exploited the changing tactical situations and played a decisive role in trying to stem the rout along the disintegrating line. It shows the SS Panzer men using tactics such as the armoured wedge, the *Panzerkeil*, and tank-destroying tactics.

The book is a captivating glimpse of a remarkable band of armoured crew men that evolved on the battlefield and were unmatched in their fighting vehicles. It reveals their successes and defeats. Even during the last months of the war as the Panzers withdrew even further across a scarred and devastated Eastern Front, it shows how units, broken down into small battle groups or *Kampfgruppen* fought to the grim death, trying to hold back the superior weight of their enemy in order to win time and save their forces from ultimate destruction.

Chapter One

BARBAROSSA 1941

The weapons associated with the Waffen-SS for the invasion of the Soviet Union on 22 June 1941 comprised a wide range of armour. Together with their Wehrmacht counterparts, there were some 3,000 tanks that assembled, together with a staggering 60,000 supporting vehicles.

This massive force was distributed among three German Army Groups. Army Group North was commanded by General Wilhelm Ritter von Leeb, who had assembled his forces in East Prussia on the Lithuanian frontier. His force provided the main spearhead for the advance on Leningrad.

Army Group Centre, commanded by General Fedor von Bock, assembled on the 1939 Polish/Russian frontier, both north and south of Warsaw. Bock's force consisted of forty-two infantry divisions of the 4th and 9th armies and *Panzergruppen* II and III. This army comprised the largest number of German infantry and Panzer divisions in all three army groups.

Army Group South, commanded by General Gerd von Rundstedt, was deployed down the longest stretch of border with Russia. The front, reaching from central Poland to the Black Sea, was held by one Panzer group, three German and two Romanian armies, plus a Hungarian motorized corps, under German command.

All the Waffen-SS divisions participated in the invasion. The 3rd SS *Totenkopf* and 4th *Polizei* divisions, which were attached to Army Group North, were tasked to advance through the Baltic States and on to Leningrad. The 2nd SS Division *Das Reich* was with Army Group Centre and headed towards Moscow, and the 1st SS *Leibstandarte Adolf Hitler* and the 5th] *Wiking* Division were with Army Group South, heading for the Ukraine and the city of Kiev.

Armour within the units of the Waffen-SS did not vary much from their operations against France more than a year earlier. The bulk of their force comprised Germany's first generations of pre-war tanks such as the Pz.Kpfw.II, III and IV. The Waffen-SS did not employ the Pz.Kpfw.I for operations against Russia, but did utilize the ailing 15cm sIG 33 (Sf) auf *Panzerkampfwagen* I Ausf B, sometimes referred to as the *Sturmpanzer* I *Bison*. This was a 15cm self-propelled gun mounted on the chassis of a Pz.Kpfw.I.

Other armoured vehicles used extensively in 1941 by the Waffen-SS comprised the *Sturmgeschutze* III, which proved indispensable to its units. Supporting these tank destroyers were the Sd.Kfz.250 and Sd.Kfz.251 armoured half-track personnel carriers. Then there were the SS flak mechanized formations which comprised batteries of flak guns mounted on half-tracks. These vehicles often in the forefront of battle comprised 2cm, 2cm quad and 3.7cm self-propelled guns.

Armoured cars also played a significant part in the Waffen-SS arsenal. Not only did they provide the mobility that was crucial to success on the battlefield, but they became quickly integrated with the daring ethos of the Waffen-SS. These vehicles were used for transporting troops to the forefront of the action, but were also used extensively for reconnaissance duties. The vehicles comprised the six-wheeled Sd.Kfz.231 series, the Horch four-wheeled Sd.Kfz.221, the Bussing-NAG eight-wheeled Sd.Kfz.231, the Sd.Kfz.234, Sd.Kfz.222, four-wheeled Sd.Kfz.260 and 261 armoured radio cars.

Many of these vehicles were integrated into armoured reconnaissance battalions, where they invariably spearheaded the Waffen-SS offensives, often with aggressive energy. The Eastern Front marked the beginning of the evolution of German armour in battle and marked the increase in the power of the tank and mobile anti-tank guns in the Waffen-SS.

A typical Panzer division contained one tank regiment of two or sometimes three *Abteilungen* totalling 150–200 tanks; two motorized rifle (*Schützen*) regiments, each of two battalions, whose infantry were carried in armoured half-tracks or similar vehicles; and a reconnaissance battalion of three companies (one motorcycle, two armoured car). The motorized infantry divisions accompanying the Panzer divisions in the *Panzergruppe* were similarly organized, but severely lacked armoured support. The divisional artillery comprised two field, one medium and one anti-tank regiment and an anti-aircraft battalion. These were all motorized and more than capable of keeping up with the fast-moving pace of the Panzers. All the components that made up a fully-fledged Panzer division comprised various half-tracks and artillery prime movers.

During the initial weeks of the invasion of Russia the Waffen-SS played a significant part in the fighting on all fronts. After a month of victorious progress, both the Waffen-SS and Wehrmacht divisions were fighting on a front 1,000 miles wide. Along the entire front German armour exploited the terrain and had progressed at considerable speed. Yet in spite of these successes the armour was thinly spread out and the bulk of the transportation still had to be undertaken by animal draught.

Nevertheless, between June and late September 1941, Waffen-SS Panzer and motorized divisions were more or less unhindered by lack of supply, difficult terrain or bad weather conditions. However, on 6 October the first snowfall of the approaching winter was reported. It melted quickly, but turned the dirt roads into quagmires and the rivers into raging torrents. The Russian autumn with its heavy rain, sleet and snow had arrived. The armoured drive east began to slow. Wheeled vehicles soon became stuck in a sea of mud and could only advance with the aid of tracked vehicles towing them. No preparations had been made for the winter and armoured units were lacking the most basic supplies for cold weather. There were no chains available for towing vehicles and no antifreeze for the engines' coolant systems. Tank crews and infantrymen alike had no proper winter protection.

In blizzards and temperatures that fell to 30 degrees below zero, exhausted tank men soon ran out of fuel and ammunition and were compelled to break off their attack within sight of Moscow. On 6 December all plans to capture the Russian capital in 1941 had to be abandoned. The *Das Reich* Division, for instance, which had fought in front of Moscow, had lost 60 per cent of its fighting strength. Further north on the Leningrad Front, the *Totenkopf* Division had not fared much better and was embroiled in heavy fighting in the region of Demyansk where its casualty rate soared.

By the end of 1941, many of the battle-weary armoured units of the Waffen-SS were no longer fit to fight. Mobile operations had ground to a halt. Fortunately for the exhausted Panzer crews and supporting half-track units, no mobile operations had been planned during the winter of 1941, let alone for 1942. In the freezing arctic temperatures, the majority of armour was pulled out of its stagnant defensive positions and transferred to France to rest, reorganize and retrain.

By 22 December only 405 tanks were operational in front of Moscow, with 780 out of action but repairable. By the end of the year, the Germans reported the loss of 2,735 tanks plus 847 replacements since 22 June. Not even 1,400 operational and damaged tanks remained of the once powerful and proud Panzer divisions.

Despite the dire situation that befell the German war machine along the Eastern Front that first winter of 1941, survival was contributed to the versatility of both the Wehrmacht and Waffen-SS armour on the battlefield. Many of the vehicles were used to transport troops from one sector of the front to another. Others assisted in towing heavy artillery or vital supplies where animal draught had failed due to terrain or the extreme arctic conditions.

(**Above**) A light vehicle hauls a PaK 35/36 anti-tank gun towards the front during the opening phase of the invasion of the Soviet Union, code-named BARBAROSSA. This vehicle belongs to the *Wiking* Division. *(NARA)*

(**Opposite**) A squad leader belonging to the *Wiking* Division can be seen here clad in his summer camouflage tunic directing his unit towards the battlefront. Behind him is a Pz.Kpfw.II. The experiences on the Eastern Front soon showed the Waffen-SS how under-gunned and under-armoured this Panzer was, and found that it could not fight effectively. *(NARA)*

(**Below**) Waffen-SS motorcycles follow two well-camouflaged Sd.Kfz.251 half-tracks along a typical dusty Russian road. As the war on the Eastern Front dragged on, this half-track became not just a half-track intended to simply transport infantry to the edge of the battlefield but also a fully-fledged fighting vehicle. *(NARA/Bender)*

(**Opposite, above**) An Sd.Kfz.232 armoured radio vehicle belonging to the *Leibstandarte* advancing along a road. This eight-wheeled vehicle was intended to be used for missions such as reconnaissance and screening. *(NARA/Bender)*

(**Opposite, below**) Here a *Leibstandarte Panzerjäger* crew are seen moving across a field. This vehicle was a converted Pz.Kpfw.I Ausf.B tank destroyer mounting a Czech 4.7cm anti-tank gun. Anti-tank battalions 521, 529, 616, 643 and 670 were equipped with 135 *Panzerjäger* Is.

(**Above**) What appears to be the Sd.Kfz.221 light armoured car. This four-wheeled vehicle armed with a 2cm cannon was used by reconnaissance battalions (*Aufklarungs-Abteilung*) of the Panzer divisions. This particular vehicle belongs to the *Totenkopf*. *(NARA)*

(**Below**) Soldiers of the *Totenkopf* can be seen here inside a Horch cross-country vehicle bound for the front in the summer of 1941. *(NARA)*

Two photographs taken along the same stretch of road inside a ruined town showing a *Totenkopf* PaK unit with their anti-tank guns on tow. During the war anti-tank weapons proved an economical and effective counter to the fire-power of Russian armour. (*NARA*)

Two photographs taken in sequence showing the Sd.Kfz.222 light armoured car belonging to the *Totenkopf* on a road. This vehicle was the second in a series of light reconnaissance vehicles. It became the standard light armoured car of the Waffen-SS and was fitted with a heavier turret but still lacked top protection other than a wire screen mesh guard which allowed grenades to roll off. (*NARA*)

The first of six photographs showing the *Leibstandarte* during operations on the Eastern Front with an Sd.Kfz.10/4 mounting a self-propelled anti-aircraft gun. A couple of the photographs show the half-track towing the Sd.Ah.51 ammunition trailer. The sides of this vehicle could be folded down so that the crew could function properly. During the early part of the war a typical anti-tank aircraft company was organized in three platoons with a total of eighteen Sd.Kfz.10/4s, twelve with guns and six carrying ammunition.

30m

Half-tracks belonging to the *Leibstandarte* can be seen here operating during the summer of 1941. Various half-tracks were used extensively by both the Wehrmacht and the Waffen-SS. They provided better cross-country mobility than a fully-wheeled tactical support vehicle. All half-tracks in the German arsenal were classified according to the metric tonnage they were designed to haul. *(NARA)*

A *Totenkopf* Sd.Kfz.221 moving along a dusty road. Note the logs attached to the front of the vehicle. This was in order to assist the vehicle if it became bogged down in a field or on a road after a downpour of rain. Conditions in Russia were often horrendous after heavy rain, bringing wheeled columns to a halt due to the ground turning into a quagmire. Note the commander standing in the cupola wearing a pair of aviator goggles in order to shield his eyes from dust particles and dirt. *(NARA)*

A *Totenkopf* commanding officer can be seen here being transported in a Horch cross-country vehicle. Two of the crew are wearing aviator goggles to protect their eyes from the endless dust particles that were thrown up by the dusty roads. (*NARA*)

A *Totenkopf* Sd.Kfz.10 hauling what appears to be a PaK 35/36 anti-tank gun. Foliage has been attached to the vehicle in order to break up its distinctive shape from both enemy ground and aerial observation. (*NARA*)

A Pz.Kpfw.I Ausf.B *Panzerjäger* belonging to a *Leibstandarte* anti-tank battalion. This vehicle was operated by a crew of three who, due to the lack of space, had to perform more than one role. In order to carry additional crew equipment or for used ammunition casings, a welded metal or wire mesh basket was added to the rear above the engine compartment. Sometimes additional storage boxes were attached to the fenders or to the rear of the vehicle, as shown in this photograph. (*NARA*)

Soldiers of *Wiking* on the march across a field with a Pz.Kpfw.III in support. The Pz.Kpfw.III saw widespread front-line service with the Waffen-SS. The first variants in the SS arsenal still retained the 5cm KwK L/42 cannon. (*NARA*)

An *SS-Sturmführer* or troop leader can be seen here conferring with his men inside an Sd.Kfz.251 command vehicle in the summer of 1941.

Leibstandarte soldiers inside a prime mover have halted on a road. Note the divisional insignia of the *Leibstandarte* painted on the rear of the half-track. *(NARA)*

Two photographs showing Sd.Kfz.10/4 half-tracks belonging to a *Totenkopf* unit. One image shows the vehicle towing an Sd.Ah.51 ammunition trailer and the other hauling the under-gunned PaK 35/36.

A prime mover hauling a FlaK 8.8cm gun towards the battlefront in the late summer of 1941. From July of that year a number of SS FlaK units steadily grew, with them receiving its first medium battery equipped with the 3.7cm guns. Additional anti-aircraft platoons and companies in their Panzer divisions also started receiving heavy FlaK guns, but that was still limited during this time. *(NARA)*

A prime mover advances across a bridge with a 15cm howitzer on tow. This vehicle belongs to the 8th Panzer Division, which operated in Army Group North along with units of the *Totenkopf* Division.

A column of vehicles belonging to *Totenkopf* crosses a bridge in the late summer. The division soon became embroiled in heavy fighting as it advanced past Demyansk to Leningrad. *(NARA)*

A shirtless *Totenkopf* crew member is seen here undertaking some maintenance to what appears to be a stationary half-track. *(NARA)*

(**Above**) A *Leibstandarte* eight-wheeled Sd.Kfz.231 heavy armoured vehicle on a road, apparently pulling a tree trunk on a chain. This vehicle was armed with the 2cm cannon and an MG 34 machine gun for local defence. *(NARA)*

(**Opposite, above**) A half-track belonging to a *Leibstandarte* unit tows a support vehicle along a muddy road. The half-track was undoubtedly the workhorse of the Eastern Front, especially along the terrible road system that plagued seemingly endless miles of terrain. Its effective towing capability ensured that troops and ordnance often got through unhindered.

(**Opposite, below**) A *Totenkopf* reconnaissance unit enters a Russian village in the winter of 1941. The vehicle leading the advance is a rear view of an Sd.Kfz.221. Behind this vehicle is an Sd.Kfz.223 (4-rad) radio vehicle. Its large rectangular antenna was mounted on four supports and could be folded down when not in use. For protection it carried an MG 34 in a small rotating turret. Both vehicles have the national flag draped over the rear for aerial recognition purposes. *(NARA)*

During the winter the front stagnated. Here in this photograph are *Totenkopf* Sd.Kfz.251 half-tracks entering a village. Due to the appalling road conditions, use of the main roads was restricted generally to priority vehicles such as tanks and half-tracks. Next in priority came the ammunition columns and fuel convoys, and then the reinforcements needed to further the advance. The nearer to the battle zones, the worse the road system became. *(NARA)*

Chapter Two

Summer and Winter Battles 1942

The New Year opened up with both the Wehrmacht and their Waffen-SS counterparts struggling for survival. Yet, despite the deteriorating situation, fighting continued mercilessly in the snow.

By early February in Army Group North, some 95,000 Wehrmacht and Waffen-SS troops and thousands of vehicles and armour had become trapped in a giant pocket which became known as the Demyansk Pocket. Throughout March fighting inside the pocket continued to rage, with SS and Wehrmacht troops trying in vain to escape it. It was not until April that a bridgehead was finally established between the soldiers in the pocket and the rest of Army Group North. The survival of the *Totenkopf* trapped inside the pocket was a great achievement and contributed significantly to the stabilization of the German position around Lake Ilmen.

Elsewhere along the Eastern Front, as the snow thawed there was a slow recovery among the units of the Waffen-SS motorized divisions. It was realized that although the weather played a key part in the stagnation of their front lines, a number of their armoured vehicles were so under-gunned and under-armoured that they had not been able to fight effectively enough. The Pz.Kpfw.II was one such vehicle that could no longer perform successfully. By early spring the *Leibstandarte*, for instance, withdrew all their remaining Pz.Kpfw.IIs from combat. Other tanks such as the Pz.Kpfw.III, which had extensively entered front-line service in the Waffen-SS, were overhauled. Some 2,516 models of the Ausf.J variant were built and many of these, mounting their 5cm KwK 39 L/160 potent long barrels, were added in large numbers to the SS Motorized Divisions of *Das Reich* and *Wiking*. The Ausf.L variant, also featuring the powerful 5cm gun but incorporating more effective spaced armour, equipped the units of the *Leibstandarte* and *Totenkopf* divisions.

The most numerous Panzer in the Waffen-SS armour was the Pz.Kpfw.IV. By March, production of the Pz.Kpfw.IV Model F2, which mounted the more lethal long-barrelled 7.5cm KwK 40 L/43 gun, entered service. These powerful tanks equipped the four SS formations that were converted into *Panzergrenadier* divisions during 1942. Later that year the Ausf.G variant came off the production line and was rushed by train to the Eastern Front. With these new variants, newly-created Panzer units of the *Leibstandarte*, *Das Reich* and *Totenkopf* divisions received significant numbers of the Ausf.G.

The year saw the most considerable amount of armour entering the Waffen-SS. Both the upgraded Pz.Kpfw.III and IV variants were to be the backbone of the Waffen-SS spearhead through Russia. It was also recognized that in 1941 SS formations lacked indigenous armoured support, where they had to constantly call on anti-tank guns and the StuG III to fight their way through Russian lines. As a result of this the StuG III had been up-armoured and re-armed with a longer-barrelled 7.5cm gun in order to give it a genuine anti-tank capability. By the spring of 1942, the StuG III was again made even more potent by mounting the longer 7.5cm StuK 40 L/43 cannon and increased frontal armour. This variant, known as the Model F, reached the Waffen-SS divisions in the late spring.

Yet in spite of the large numbers of tanks and assault guns entering the realms of the Waffen-SS arsenal, armoured crews had found that their forces were at times increasingly vulnerable to Soviet counter-thrusts. Along the thinly-stretched lines crews often called for more and more mobile anti-tank fire-power. As a result, the Germans developed the Marder series, which converted relegated light tanks into tank-hunters or *Panzerjägers*.

Manufacturing of the *Panzerjäger* 38(t) Marder III went into production at the end of March, and within weeks the vehicle saw its debut with the Waffen-SS on the Eastern Front. Crews soon reported its tactical worth as it was more than capable of destroying Soviet T-34 tanks.

The success of the Marder III series quickly led to the development and production of the Marder II, which was a converted Pz.Kpfw II initially mounting a 7.62cm PaK 36. The *Leibstandarte*, *Das Reich*, *Totenkopf* and *Wiking* divisions became the first Waffen-SS formations to receive both the Marder II and III. These tank-hunters extensively served with the SS divisional anti-tank battalions and proved very successful in countering Russian armour.

The success of the Marder series on the thinly-manned Eastern Front meant that troops and tanks alike became increasingly reliant on the defensive power of these fast-moving armoured tank-hunters to ward off and destroy the ever-growing numbers of Russian tanks. As a result, this led to another vehicle known as the *Wespe* (Wasp) being produced. The *Wespe* mounted the standard 10.5cm field howitzer on the chassis of a Pz.Kpfw.II. It did not take long before these vehicles appeared on the Eastern Front, serving in the armoured artillery battalions of the SS Panzer divisions. At first, the battalions comprised three light batteries of four *Wespe* vehicles. However, when the new Hummel or Bumble-Bee was introduced in late 1942, the composition changed and comprised two light batteries of six *Wespe* and one heavy battery equipped with six Hummels.

The Hummel was a self-propelled gun armed with the powerful 15cm field howitzer mounted on the chassis of either a Pz.Kpfw.III or IV. It was allocated to both Wehrmacht and Waffen-SS divisions, which illustrated the demand required by the Germans, irrespective of whether they were elite formations or not, to counter the Russian armoured threat.

As for units of the Waffen-SS, they were totally aware of what was required of them, and it was primarily for this reason that their divisions saw further expansion of their armoured arsenal. It also marked further expansion of their divisions. By the second half of 1942, an increasing number of foreign troops, many of whom were not volunteers, began entering the ranks. The 7th SS Volunteer Mountain Division (*Gebirgsjäger*) *Prinz Eugen* was recruited along with the SS Cavalry Brigade, which was used as the cadre in the formation of the 8th SS Cavalry Division *Florian Geyer*. Other foreign units comprised Flemings (Belgians) in the *Freiwilligen Legion Flandern*, the *Freikorps Danmark* consisting of Danish volunteers, the *Freiwilligen Legion Norwegen* manned by Norwegian SS recruits and the *Finnische Freiwilligen-Bataillon der Waffen-SS*, which was eventually attached to the 5th *Wiking* Division. There were also *Volksdeutscher* 'ethnic German' recruits from Hungary and Romania together with a few Norwegians that formed the 6th SS Division *Nord*, which was later to become a mountain division.

As for the premier Waffen-SS divisions, their units had became fully motorized with each division having a Panzer regiment. Before the end of the year the Panzer-equipped units were officially redesignated as *SS-Panzergrenadier-Divisionen* or armoured infantry divisions.

It would be these 'classic' SS divisions comprising the *Leibstandarte*, *Das Reich*, *Totenkopf*, *Polizei*, *Wiking* and *Nord* that were to play a significant part in the war on the Eastern Front. With their new armour they were required to make great sacrifices in the name of their beloved Führer while trying to spearhead their forces across the vast expanses of the Soviet Union, attempting not only to capture important ground but to combat a growing enemy.

What appears to be an Sd.Kfz.6/2 mounting a 3.7cm FlaK 36. This vehicle belongs to the *Leibstandarte* and has caused some interest among the local population. *(NARA)*

An Sd.Kfz.251 advances along a road while two reconnaissance aircraft return from the front lines. All across the front both troops and tanks had ground to a halt in the arctic conditions. The extreme winter of late 1941 and early 1942 had caused both the Wehrmacht and Waffen-SS armoured columns serious delays. As a result much of the front stagnated until the spring thaw of 1942, delaying the conquest of Russia by months. BARBAROSSA had been a success in terms of the vast distances that had been travelled, but coupled with growing enemy resistance and the Russian winter, it had failed to achieve its objective. *(NARA)*

An Sd.Kfz.7/1 mounting a 2cm FlaK 38 is clearly shown here in a field with its crew preparing the weapon for a fire mission against an enemy target. Interestingly the sides of the vehicle remain upright, which suggests this vehicle might require quick relocation to another position. *(NARA)*

Soldiers belonging to a *Wiking* unit have hitched a lift on board a Pz.Kpfw.III during spring operations. The division had advanced through Galicia and had successfully fought for the bridgehead across the Dnieper River. Later, the division took part in the heavy fighting for Rostov-on-Don before reluctantly withdrawing to the Mius River line in late 1941. Following the spring thaw the division was ordered to take part in Army Group South's offensive, known as Case Blue, which was aimed at capturing the city of Stalingrad and the Baku oilfields. *(NARA)*

(**Above**) Here *Leibstandarte* troops are assisting a support vehicle across uneven ground during spring operations. Even during the initial stages of the invasion of Russia the supply situation was exacerbated by the almost non-existence of proper roads throughout the Soviet Union. Half-tracks and other tracked vehicles were utilized to help speed up the supply of ammunition and other equipment desperately needed at the front. *(NARA)*

(**Opposite, above**) A *Leibstandarte* motorcycle combination probably on a reconnaissance mission pauses during its advance inside a town that has been ravaged by fighting. They can both be seen wearing the double-breasted rubberized motorcycle coat. The garment was waterproof and was worn with army canvas leather issue gloves or cloth mittens, with overshoe leggings or army boots. One of the hazards of travelling by motorcycle, especially in the Soviet Union, was the lack of good quality roads for vehicles. Motorcyclists that decided to avoid the roads and travel across country often found this a perilous undertaking and the casualty rate among them was inevitably high. *(NARA)*

(**Opposite, below**) Half-tracks are seen here spread out across a field in order to minimize the threat of an enemy aerial attack. Note the number of dead Soviet troops sprawled out in the field. *(NARA)*

SS troops have obviously dismounted from this stationary Sd.Kfz.251 half-track, but have taken immediate cover on the road due to enemy activity in the area. *(NARA)*

Wiking troops have hitched a lift on board what appears to be a Pz.Kpfw.III. Carrying troops to the forward edge of the battlefield by tank was a common occurrence on the Eastern Front. The vast distances over which the soldiers had to march had a noticeable impact on the men, both mentally and physically. *(NARA)*

The first of six photographs, some of which were taken in sequence, show the *Wiking* Division operating with their Pz.Kpfw.III in the summer of 1942. It was during this period that *Wiking* along with the *Leibstandarte* had its Panzer battalions equipped with the more potent long-barrelled 5cm KwK 39 L/60 gun. Later that year the battalions received more Pz.Kpfw.IIIs which retained the same cannon but incorporated more effective spaced armour. (*NARA*)

R14

Wiking grenadiers rest beside a Pz.Kpfw.III during summer operations. (*NARA*)

A Pz.Kpfw.III can be seen here, more than likely operating in the Crimea. The tank is armed with the 5cm KwK 39 L/60 gun. *(NARA)*

An Sd.Kfz.251/1 Ausf.C mounting the PaK 35/36 can be seen here halted in a field. Two Russian soldiers have just been captured; one of them appears to be aided by their comrade following an injury. *(NARA)*

A *Leibstandarte* 28/32cm Nebelwerfer 41 launcher towed by an Sd.Kfz.10/1 half-track. Rockets began to be issued in 1941 to a new elite rocket-projector group of *Nebeltruppe*. These groups served in independent army rocket-launcher battalions and later regiments and brigades. Small Waffen-SS battalions began receiving these weapons, but it was not until 1943 that the first SS rocket-launcher battalions were properly equipped with the fearsome 15cm NBW 41. *(NARA)*

A knocked-out StuG III. On the battlefield these vehicles were crucial for mobile fire support to the thinly-stretched and greatly outnumbered Waffen-SS, for whom armoured reserves were scarce. Again and again these vehicles were used in an anti-tank role which deprived SS grenadiers of the fire support they needed. As a consequence, many StuG IIIs became vulnerable to enemy anti-tank fire and were destroyed. *(NARA)*

A 15cm howitzer is being halted here by a half-track vehicle during operations in Army Group North. This artillery piece belongs to the SS *Gebirgsjäger* Regiment 11 *Reinhard Heydrich* of the 6th SS Division *Nord*. (*NARA*)

During the winter of 1942 SS grenadiers are seen here on the march being supported by a StuG III. In combat the StuG III proved to be a robust and invaluable anti-tank weapon. Although it suffered the disadvantage of a rotating turret, this drawback was less of a problem in a defensive role, which the Waffen-SS increasingly employed on the front lines from 1943. (*NARA*)

Chapter Three

Fighting Withdrawal in the South 1943

On the Eastern Front the Red Army offensives of late 1942 and early 1943 compelled the German forces to grudgingly go back on the defensive. Already their armour was stretched to the limit. Even the introduction of the new Tiger tank which had been given to the three premier Waffen-SS divisions struggled to further augment their combat effectiveness.

By February 1943, with nothing but a chain of defeats, Hitler was determined to prevent a deep withdrawal and utilize his elite Waffen-SS divisions with their Tigers to block the Red Army's drive past the city of Kharkov. With the Soviets already intoxicated by their victory at Stalingrad, Hitler was resolute in not allowing Kharkov to fall into enemy hands. The task of carrying out the battle for Kharkov was left to the newly-formed *I SS Panzer-Corps* comprising the *Leibstandarte*, *Das Reich* and *Totenkopf* divisions, which had been rushed to the Eastern Front from France. The *Leibstandarte* and *Das Reich* were under the command of *SS-Obergruppenführer* Paul 'Papa' Hausser's *I SS Panzer-Corps*. Hausser's SS Corps were ordered to fight to the grim death inside the rubble-strewn city, but following days of continuous combat they were compelled to evacuate the city, much to the fury of Hitler.

On 4 March, determined to retake Kharkov, the 4th Panzer Army joined forces with the *I SS Panzer-Corps* and launched a massive attack with *Das Reich* penetrating the outskirts of the city. To the north the *Leibstandarte*'s Panzer-Regiment I and II smashed their way into Kharkov. Fierce fighting ensued and as Soviet forces escaped onto the Kharkov-Belgorod road, *Totenkopf* troops were there ready to annihilate them.

The victory at Kharkov was now complete, but the capture of the city had come at a heavy price in blood with some 12,000 soldiers killed. With Kharkov retaken, Hitler now confidently planned a new offensive against the Kursk salient. Here the Führer was confronted with a very tempting strategic opportunity that would, he predicted, yield him victory.

For the offensive, twenty-one Panzer divisions, including four Waffen-SS divisions and two *Panzergrenadier* divisions, were prepared for what was known as Operation *ZITADELLE* in the Kursk salient. For this massive attack the *Panzerwaffe* were able to muster in early July 17 divisions and 2 brigades with no fewer than 1,715 Panzers and 147 *Sturmegeschutz* III (StuG) assault guns. Each division averaged some ninety-eight Panzers and self-propelled anti-tank guns. The new Pz.Kpfw.V Panther made its debut, despite its production problems.

These new Panthers comprising some 250 Ausf.D variants were tasked to spearhead the attack through the Kursk salient. The three SS Panzer divisions committed to Kursk; the *Leibstandarte*, *Das Reich* and *Totenkopf* were not given any Panthers for the battle. However, they did have the mighty Tigers, which played, as they had done at Kharkov, a key role in the battle. The *I SS Panzer-Corps* fielded forty-one Tigers.

With these armoured vehicles as the backbone of the driving force through the salient, both Wehrmacht and Waffen-SS units were determined to rejuvenate their blitzkrieg tactics. However, unknown to the German command, immense preparations had gone into constructing the Soviet defences, which meant that German armour was never ever going to succeed in penetrating into the strategic depths of the Red Army fortifications with any overriding success.

When the attack was finally unleashed in the pre-dawn light of 5 July 1943, the Germans were stunned by the dogged defence of their Soviet foe. The battle was unlike any other engagement they had previously encountered. A German grenadier wrote:

> The Red Army soldiers refused to give up. Nor did they panic in the face of our roaring Tiger tanks. The Soviets were cunning in every way. They allowed our tanks to rumble past their well-camouflaged foxholes and then sprang out to deal with the German grenadiers following in its wake. Constantly our tanks and assault guns had to turn back to relieve the stranded and often exhausted grenadiers.

Within only a matter of days, the Red Army had slowly ground down many of the advanced armoured units, which consequently threw the German offensive timetable off schedule. Through sheer weight of Soviet strength and stubborn combat along an ever-extending front, the German mobile units were finally forced to a standstill.

The losses that the Germans sustained at Kursk were so immense that it undoubtedly led to the German army taking the first steps of its slow retreat back towards Germany. The Russians had managed to destroy no fewer than thirty divisions, seven of which were Panzers.

After Kursk, the *Leibstandarte* was withdrawn and sent to Italy, while the *Das Reich* and *Totenkopf* divisions remained heavily engaged on the Eastern Front. The reverberations caused by the defeat at Kursk meant that these Waffen-SS divisions were overstretched, plugging holes in the front and supporting Wehrmacht units cut off or trapped. Yet despite the deteriorating situation, the SS tank men felt that they were now duty-bound to improvise with what they had at their disposal and try to maintain themselves in the field, and in doing so they hoped to wear down the enemy's offensive capacity. Stiff defensive action was now the stratagem placed upon the divisions, but a number of units lacked sufficient reinforcements and the strength of their armoured units dwindled steadily as they tried to hold back the Russian might.

Across the whole Eastern Front units were fighting a frenzied battle of attrition. Massed Soviet artillery bombardments would sweep the German lines and inflict considerable casualties on both infantry and armoured vehicles. The Russians were determined not to allow the Germans any respite and launched a massive attack, overrunning Field Marshal von Manstein's positions on the Mius River. Both *Totenkopf* and *Das Reich* were rushed north to protect von Manstein's left flank. Although these SS units distinguished themselves with their bravery, they could only manage to stem the Red Army for short periods of time. Along the banks of the Mius River SS armour had blunted Soviet forces and sent enemy units reeling back across the water.

However, by mid-August 1943, the Russians had wrenched open a huge gap in the German lines west of Kursk, once again threatening to re-take the important industrial city of Kharkov. The *Das Reich*, *Totenkopf* and *Wiking* divisions were immediately thrown into battle to prevent the loss of the city. Although all these combat formations were weakened by the *ZITADELLE* (Operation CITADEL) disaster, they were still a formidable fighting force. The city itself had only been recaptured by the Waffen-SS in March 1943, and now it was the Red Army's turn to launch a massive pincer attack to take it back again.

Within days of the SS redeployment to Kharkov the Russian 53rd Army driving from the north and the 57th Army advancing from the south attacked the city with all their might. Almost immediately the SS troops crashed into action and defended Kharkov with every last drop of blood.

On 20 August, the *Totenkopf* and *Grossdeutschland* divisions joined hands to close the gap west of the city. However, by this stage of the battle both divisions were running out of ammunition and were already relying heavily on artillery to undertake the main burden of defending their positions. The high consumption of ammunition in the last month had put serious strain on all the German combat formations in and around Kharkov. In many units daily requirements in artillery and tank ammunition were down to half the normal capacity required to sustain a force of such magnitude in a defensive position. However, despite these problems, von Manstein still thought he might be able to hold Kharkov by using *Das Reich* in a counter-attack. The soldiers of *Das Reich* were to throw everything they could possibly muster against the Soviets, but when they arrived in the 6th Corps' zone of operations, they found that the artillerymen, after firing their last rounds, were abandoning their guns and fighting as infantry.

Fighting around the city was heavy. In just one day fighting SS anti-tank gunners knocked out almost 200 Soviet tanks. The *Das Reich* Panther battalion, which first saw heavy combat on 22 August, destroyed fifty-three Russian tanks. The next day, just west of Kharkov, a Panther platoon broke up a Russian tank assault and one Panther destroyed seven tanks. On 24 August the *6.SS.Panzer-Kompanie*, newly-supplied with the latest Panzer IVs, battled sixty Russian T-34 tanks between Udy-Bogens and Orkan just south-west of the city and knocked out twenty-nine of them. In the ten-day battle that raged around Kharkov, the *Das Reich* Division alone had scored 463 armoured kills.

Totenkopf and *Wiking* were equally impressive, and fought a series of skilful duels against numerically superior enemy forces. Again and again they showed their worth in the field of action. In spite of serious losses in men and matériel, the troops continued fighting with all the ruthlessness and élan that made them such an efficient and lethal weapon of war.

Through the latter part of August the SS continued to score some outstanding successes in localized combats with Russian armoured units. However, with acute shortages in men and equipment, the situation deteriorated day by day. Despite frantic calls from commanders appealing for evacuation from the city, Hitler sent out an order that Kharkov be held under all circumstances and demanded the most severe measures against any units that failed to execute their assigned missions. Both Wehrmacht and Waffen-SS units were forced to undertake their Führer's futile exercise of holding Kharkov to the grim death.

However, as developments rapidly deteriorated and the hard-pressed armoured units became ground down against numerically superior forces, Hitler became increasingly worried that another Stalingrad would soon develop. By early September he grudgingly decided to go ahead and allow the order to pull the troops out of the doomed city. The evacuation of Kharkov was undertaken by a spirited withdrawal by the Waffen-SS towards the Dnieper River. Here the SS managed to halt the Russian onslaught towards the river, allowing von Manstein's forces to retreat and redeploy. Both *Totenkopf* and *Das Reich* had helped to divert a major disaster in the area and given von Manstein a little time to reorganize the front from the inevitable disaster that was looming. Both the SS divisions, together with the elite arm of *Groß-deutschland*, covered the general retreat to the river before themselves retiring to its western bank. Von Manstein was very aware that his army group could no longer hold the Donetz Line and therefore sought to withdraw and regroup his forces across the Dnieper. Altogether some 68 German divisions – 1,250,000 men and more than 2,000 tanks of Army Group South – were tasked with holding the river line at all costs. Opposing them, however, was a Red Army almost double in size and furnished with plenty of reserves in fresh men and equipment.

The Dnieper was the second-largest Russian river and the strongest natural defence line in western Russia. Fortified and adequately manned, it would have been ideally defensible, but the condition of Army Group South in September 1943 was such that the river was only modestly capable of affording any natural protection and delaying the Soviet advance. When troops crossed the river during their withdrawal from Kharkov they were dismayed to find none of the impregnable fortifications constructed.

Here along the Dnieper there was still no respite from the fury of the Russian advance. In the first ten days of October the Red Army launched an attack against German positions in the great bend of the river between Kremenchuk and Zaporozhye. The attack began with a massive artillery preparation that pounded the German bridgehead. In less than an hour the Germans had counted some 15,000 shell bursts in their sector. German batteries replied in kind as far as they were able, but the main attack would fall on the infantry. By 15 October, the Russian 2nd Ukrainian Front, with a total of six armies, bulldozed its way through and crossed the river.

During the next few days they poured divisions across the river and tore open the German-held front between the *8.Armee* and the left wing of the I Panzer Army. On 18 October troops took Piatikhatki, 35 miles south of the Dnieper, and cut off the main railway lines to Dnepropetrovsk and Krivoy Rog. Russian forces were now driving straight for Krivoy Rog, the supply and communications centre for Army Group South. The city of Krivoy Rog contained the supply and ammunition dumps for the area, and the locomotives there were a vital asset for supply to the army group.

Von Manstein was determined that he could not allow the loss of Krivoy Rog and scraped together what he could muster to stem the Russian onslaught. He managed to find six weakened armoured divisions, including the *Totenkopf*. Even the units of the SS were hard pressed and did not receive the ample supplies of fresh men and armour that had been promised. Instead they were put into line on the right flank of the Soviet advance. What followed was a massive counter-thrust with Wehrmacht and Waffen-SS troops using all available reserves and resources to bitterly contest the Russian advance. In the bloody battle that ensued, the Germans, at great cost in men and matériel, managed to break up two Russian armoured corps and nine rifle divisions. The Red Army lost more than 300 tanks and 5,000 prisoners. The remaining Russian forces in the area staggered back towards the Dnieper, allowing the exhausted German combat formations to temporarily stabilize the front.

The troops were made fully aware of the significance of holding the vital city of Krivoy Rog, and the outcome would be the deciding factor in the future operations of Army Group South in the Crimea.

Meanwhile, further north along the Dnieper River soldiers of *Das Reich* had been trying to prevent large numbers of enemy forces from consolidating control areas west of the river. Both SS troopers and Red Army forces had been battling throughout late September and October, trying to stop the Russians establishing a bridgehead. *Der Führer* Regiment had seized the town of Greben, but at great cost. Only 500 soldiers were left in its ranks. Still undeterred by the losses, *Das Reich* continued to fight a number of inconclusive battles in the region which saw its regiments and battalions become even further depleted.

Ominously, throughout the weeks that followed, the German front lines were pulled further westwards with *Das Reich* defending, attacking and counter-attacking as the situation demanded. A number of the battles that were fought in this sector of the front were owed to the efforts of the SS armoured units, but they paid a high price in blood.

Leibstandarte troops wearing their new Waffen-SS winter anoraks grey side out can be seen here next to an Sd.Kfz.10 half-track in the snow during the winter of 1943. (*NARA*)

A 15cm schwere *Panzerhaubitze auf Geschsützwagen* III-IV Sf Hummel during operations in the Ukraine during the winter of 1943.

A battery of *Wespes* during the winter of 1943.

Two photographs taken in sequence showing whitewashed Sd.Kfz.251/1 Ausf.C more than likely in the Kharkov area in February or March 1943. Note the half-track with a national flag draped over the front engine cover for aerial recognition. Winter-clad SS grenadiers are seen wearing their insulated anoraks grey side out, apart from what appears to be their commander in a white animal skin coat. *(NARA)*

A column of 1-ton Sd.Kfz.10s can be seen here advancing towards the battlefront. The leading half-track is towing what appears to be a 5cm PaK 38. On board this vehicle are metal ammunition boxes which carried four rounds for the PaK gun. Strapped to the side of the fender is a 20-litre 'jerry can'. *(NARA)*

During a reconnaissance mission and a *Das Reich* commanding officer can be seen standing on the frontal structure of his Sd.Kfz.251 to get a better view of the area ahead. He holds a pair of Zeiss 6 × 10 binoculars. Note the 2m rod radio antenna and the MG 34 mounted at the front with splinter shield. *(NARA)*

Two soldiers, more than likely *Das Reich* machine-gunners, can be seen here taking cover in a field flanked by an advancing Pz.Kpfw.III. In the distance are what appear to be Pz.Kpfw.IVs complete with side-skirts or *Schürzen*, which were more resistant to anti-tank rifle fire. (*NARA*)

An interesting photograph showing a Pz.Kpfw.III belonging to the *Das Reich* Division with captured Russian prisoners on board. (*NARA*)

A well-camouflaged Marder II *Panzerjäger* flanked by a Pz.Kpfw.III Marder II, which was a converted Pz.Kpfw.II, initially mounting a 7.62cm PaK 36. The *Leibstandarte*, *Das Reich*, *Totenkopf* and *Wiking* divisions became the first Waffen-SS formations to receive the Marder II. *(Bender)*

Another photograph showing the Marder II. The *Panzerjäger* is well camouflaged in order to help break up its distinctive shape. *(Bender)*

304

(**Left**) A Pz.Kpfw.II belonging to the *Wiking* Division has halted in a field. Both the commander and the grenadier, who is more than likely a troop leader and armed with an MP 38/40, are surveying the terrain ahead. *(NARA)*

(**Right**) A *Wiking* Pz.Kpfw.III commander can be seen here surveying the battlefield ahead while standing in his cupola. The hatch doors are open to release the heat that was generated inside the tank during summer operations. *(NARA)*

(**Below**) What appears to be an Sd.Kfz.231 (8-rad) with soldiers hitching a lift on the engine deck. The Sd.Kfz.231 was a heavy reconnaissance vehicle which, with its all-round independent steering, gave the machine an unprecedented level of maoeuvrability on all kinds of roads. *(NARA)*

By 1943 the *Wespe* had become a popular mobile artillery vehicle. It was armed with a 10.5cm le.FH 18/2 L/28 gun and protected by a lightly-armoured superstructure on the chassis of a Pz.Kpfw.II. This vehicle served in both Wehrmacht and Waffen-SS armoured artillery battalions, but many were lost as a result of being lightly-armoured.

Three photographs showing a new Tiger tank belonging to *Totenkopf* loaded and chocked on special flatbed railway cars destined for another part of the Eastern Front. These Tigers were attached to the new heavy Panzer battalions. In order for these transport wagons to be moved by train, special loading platforms had been constructed. This allowed loads to be entrained and detrained quickly. Moving vehicles by rail became a common requirement in the Waffen-SS in 1943. It enabled the Panzer divisions to move from one front to another quickly and effectively without incurring wear and tear. Note that the Tigers still retain their factory colour of a dark yellow sand base. *(NARA)*

Often when vehicles came off the production line they were rushed into service and transported to the front in their factory colours. These *Totenkopf* Tigers are receiving their camouflage coating at the front. They are being sprayed in an interesting summer camouflage pattern of dark yellow with red-brown and olive-green wavy lines. These colours were often seen at the Battle of Kursk in July 1943. *(NARA)*

Three photographs taken in sequence showing the completed summer camouflage scheme of these Tigers before they were put back on the front line in the summer of 1943. *(NARA)*

Here a crew can be seen with their Tiger tank during the opening phase of the Kursk offensive, Operation CITADEL, in early July 1943. In front of the Soviet defensive fortress at Kursk stood the cream of all the German combat formations.

Two Tigers and a StuG III can be seen here during the Kursk offensive. This armour belongs to the II.SS.Panzer-Corps which comprised three premier Waffen-SS divisions: *Leibstandarte*, *Das Reich* and the *Totenkopf*.

A Tiger tank can be seen here moving along a track while SS grenadiers clad in their summer smocks march in a different direction. Some 102 Tiger tanks were used at Kursk, but were in fact facing an even greater enemy, coupled with almost impregnable defensive belts.

At Kursk a Tiger crew prepares their vehicle for action. Note the national flag attached to the rear of the engine deck for aerial recognition. In front of the Soviet defensive fortress stood the Waffen-SS combat formations. These elite units, comprising the II.SS.Panzer-Corps commanded by *SS-Obergruppenführer* Paul Hausser, formed part of the 4th Panzer Army. The corps comprised the three premier Waffen-SS divisions which had a line strength of 390 of the latest tanks and 104 assault guns between them, including 42 of the Army Group's Tigers. At their starting positions, the three SS divisions covered a sector that was 12 miles wide. The *Totenkopf* occupied the left flank of the advance, the *Leibstandarte* was in the centre and *Das Reich* held the right. *(NARA)*

Seven photographs showing Tiger tanks in action during the Kursk offensive. During the climax of the battle both the *Totenkopf* and *Leibstandarte* heavily attacked, while *Das Reich* remained on the defensive using Tiger tanks extensively, repelling a number of armour and infantry attacks. Although Russian losses in both men and equipment far exceeded those of the Germans, their losses could be replaced. German losses, however, except where armour could be recovered, were total. Within less than a week of *ZITADELLE* being unleashed, both sides had lost several hundred tanks and thousands of troops. While the Red Army was able to repair and replace its losses, the SS divisions had to struggle on with what they had left at their disposal. Slowly the II-SS Panzer-Corps was being ground down in a battle of attrition. The Russians had committed no fewer than seven corps, with more than 850 tanks and SU-85 assault guns. *(NARA)*

S13

S21

Two photographs showing a number of Panzers, mainly the Pz.Kpfw.IV, belonging to the *Leibstandarte* can be seen here on the advance during the Kursk offensive. By 13 July, the II.SS.Panzer-Corps was unable to make any further progress and poor ground conditions were hampering its re-supply efforts. *(NARA)*

A *Leibstandarte* tank commander can be seen here standing inside his cupola with his tank headphones, surveying the battlefield through a pair of binoculars. (*NARA*)

Halted in a field are SS grenadiers and a Tiger tank. By 13 July Russian forces at Kursk had managed to drive back *Das Reich* in the area of the Rakovo-Kruglik road and recaptured Hill 247 and the town of Berezovka. The following day, *Totenkopf* was forced out of its bridgehead on the northern bank of the Psel River, while further east *Das Reich* had made limited progress, capturing the town of Belenichino. (*NARA*)

A photograph taken from the side of what appears to be a Marder tank destroyer. Black smoke can be seen rising in the distance. *(NARA)*

A StuG III Ausf.G variant complete with side skirts advances along a road with two grenadiers hitching a lift. Note that part of a track link has been bolted to the frontal plate of the vehicle for additional armoured protection. *(NARA)*

Grenadiers on the march supported by a StuG III. In the distance a number of other armoured vehicles can be seen spread across a field. *(NARA)*

Grenadiers belonging to the *Wiking* Division are seen marching towards the front supported by Pz.Kpfw.IIIs.

Three photographs showing the StuG III at Kursk during the latter part of the offensive. By 15 July the Russian offensive to the north of the Kursk salient was threatening the 9th Army rear and as a result it was forced to begin a planned withdrawal westwards to avoid encirclement. Following its withdrawal, almost all offensive action around Prokhorovka ceased and German forces in the area went over to the defensive. *(NARA)*

(**Above**) Out in a field during summer operations is a stationary Sd.Kfz.251 armoured personnel carrier belonging to a unit of the *Leibstandarte*. (NARA)

(**Opposite**) The rear of a Pz.Kpfw.III, which has halted in a field. One of the crew members, probably the driver, and the commander can be seen surveying the situation ahead. A vehicle appears to be on fire. (NARA)

(**Below**) A Marder on the advance in a field. By 1943 these *Panzerjäger-Abteilungen* of the Panzer divisions were found both in the Wehrmacht and the Waffen-SS, as well as several Luftwaffe units. However, the Marder's survivability was flawed by the combination of a high silhouette and open-top fighting compartment which made them vulnerable to indirect artillery and anti-tank fire, aircraft strafing and grenades. (NARA)

Three photographs showing *Wiking* grenadiers clearing a dirt road for a Pz.Kpfw.III. (*NARA*)

A column of Pz.Kpfw.IIIs belonging to the *Wiking* Division can be seen here halted on a road. The crews of these tanks appear in quite good humour and smile for the camera. *(NARA)*

A captured Russian T-34 tank has been requisitioned into a *Leibstandarte* unit. For identification purposes a national cross has been painted on the side of the turret and a black painted swastika applied on a white background on the top side of the commander's hatch. *(NARA)*

Two crew members of an Sd.Kfz.222 light armoured car belonging to the 11th SS Volunteer *Panzergrenadier* Division *Nordland* (11 *SS-Freiwilligen-Panzergrenadier-Division Nordland*) can be seen here in their vehicle. The wire screen mesh guard can be seen open. This was a Waffen-SS division recruited from foreign volunteers and conscripts in early 1943. (*NARA*)

A column of *Schwimmwagen* vehicles is halted here in a village. They belong to the *SS-Panzergrenadier-Regiment 24 Danmark* of the 11 *SS-Freiwilligen-Panzergrenadier-Division Nordland*. The *Nordland* Division had two *Panzergrenadier* regiments which were given regimental titles of reference to the location from which the majority of the regiment's recruits came. The *SS-Panzergrenadier Regiment 23 Norge* were from Norway and the *SS-Panzergrenadier Regiment 24 Danmark* were recruits from Denmark. (NARA)

Grenadiers belonging to the *SS-Panzergrenadier Regiment 24 Danmark* are seen here crossing a dirt road to take cover behind a StuG III. Initially the division began combat operations against Yugoslav partisans in September 1943. The *Nordland* Division, along with the rest of the III SS Panzer Corps, was then sent to the front near Leningrad and put into action against the Red Army which was trying to break the German encirclement of the city. *(NARA)*

Grenadiers belonging to the *SS-Kavallerie* Division are seen here on board a StuG III. This division was officially known as the 8th SS Cavalry Division *Florian Geyer*. It was formed in 1942 from a cadre of the SS Cavalry Brigade. The newly-created division was sent to the Eastern Front where it saw extensive fighting in the Rzhev and Orel sectors in central Russia until the spring of 1943 in the Army Group Centre rear area. *(NARA)*

A motorcycle cavalry unit belonging to the SS-*Kavallerie* Division during what probably is a reconnaissance mission in the summer of 1944. The division put together a Panzer Reconnaissance Battalion when it was sent to Hungary in late 1943. *(NARA)*

A StuG.III attached to the SS-*Kavallerie* Division advances along a dirt track. This is more than likely operating in Hungary in 1944 where both *Panzerjäger* and *Sturmgeschütz* battalions were combined in operations against partisan groups. *(NARA)*

Two photographs taken in sequence showing a crew member of a StuG III of the *SS-Kavallerie Division* conferring with one of his cavalry comrades on horseback. *(NARA)*

Four photographs taken of the same *SS-Kavallerie Division SS-Sturmgeschütz-Batterie* operating on the Eastern Front. The 8th *SS-Sturmgeschütz-Abteilung* (assault gun) was equipped with the 1st Company comprising twelve StuGs along with the 2nd Company comprising Pz.Kpfw.IVs and the 3rd equipped with Pz.Kpfw.III Ausf.J variants. From its conception in 1942 the division saw heavy fighting around Smolensk, Rzhev, Orel and Dujepr, culminating with the liberation and occupation of Hungary where it met its final destruction in 1944. *(NARA)*

Chapter Four

Winter and Summer Battles 1943–44

The winter of 1943 opened up with an exasperating series of deliberations for the *Panzerwaffe*. Much of its concerns were to do with overcoming the awesome might of the Red Army with what little they had available at their disposal. Yet in October and November 1943 only five Panzer divisions and one SS Panzer division were sent as replacements on the Eastern Front. Of these, only the *Leibstandarte* and 1st Panzer Division were at full strength with two battalions totalling some 180 tanks. The 14th, 24th and 25th Panzer divisions had about 100 tanks and assault guns in one single battalion. During the winter of 1943 all units on the Eastern Front averaged 2,000 tanks, of which only 800 were regarded as combat-ready at any one time. The SS did receive a high proportion of tanks, artillery and assault guns, but this was in stark contrast to the enormous volume of armaments being produced by the Russians. Their new role as the so-called 'fire brigades', being shuttled from one danger spot to another to dampen down heavy Russian attacks, typified their position during late 1943. In total there were seven SS divisions that became Hitler's emergency 'fire brigade', and it was in October 1943 that these seven crack SS *Panzergrenadier* divisions – *Leibstandarte Adolf Hitler*, *Das Reich*, *Totenkopf*, *Wiking*, *Hohenstaufen*, *Frundsberg* and *Hitlerjugend* – were redesignated as SS Panzer divisions.

It was for this reason that Hitler was forced to order the return of the *Leibstandarte* from Italy. By November 1943, barely three months after departing, the division, now completely rested and re-equipped with the latest tanks and assault guns, returned to its old fighting ground in the east.

The SS Division arrived on the battlefield south of Kiev in early November 1943. It was to be the main attacking division in the 4th Panzer Division and was to strike northwards towards Kiev, which had already fallen into enemy hands. When the attack opened on 13 November the *Leibstandarte* formed two *Kampfgruppen*. The left arm went via Rogosna, crossed the Kamenka and Unova rivers and cut the Fastov-Brodel railway line south of Mochnaczka. The right group drove north-eastwards, passed Pistachki, captured Trylissy, then established bridgeheads across the Kamenka River, and then drove with all its might towards Fastov. It was here at

Fastov that the first major tank battles of the offensive were unleashed. The new Panzer ace, *SS-Obersturmführer* Michael Wittmann, destroyed six Soviet tanks and five anti-tank guns before driving to the rear echelon to refuel and take on more ammunition. Returning to battle following lunch, he then destroyed a further ten tanks and another seven guns. SS grenadiers were then able to reach the Kiev-Zhitomir highway. The town of Brusilov was then captured and the SS advance temporarily continued. Inevitably though, the SS Panzer thrusts soon slowed and then halted. Operations in the area ceased on 23 November when warm weather turned the previously frozen roads into a quagmire.

In *Das Reich*'s area of operations the division also fought well with distinction to detain the Russians from marching across the western Ukraine. However, the unrelenting fighting had proved to be more than even *Das Reich* could endure. Consequently, by December 1943, it was no longer capable of carrying out the tasks given to a full-strength division and orders were issued to create a *Kampfgruppen* from the units still fit for action. On 17 December the Panzer *Kampfgruppen* was constructed out of the *Panzergrenadier* Regiment *Das Reich*. The *Kampfgruppen* consisted of the 1st *Bataillon Deutschland* and 2nd *Bataillon der Führer* regiments. Two companies constituted the Panzer battalion *Das Reich*, and also on strength were the reconnaissance battalion, artillery, Nebelwerfers, pioneers, a heavy infantry gun company and two self-propelled companies. The strength of *Kampfgruppe Das Reich*, as it was now called, would remain on the Eastern Front while the remaining elements returned to Germany for a refit.

While *Kampfgruppen Das Reich* dug in around the deep woods south-east of Radomyshl-Guta Sabelozkaya, near Krivoy Rog the *Totenkopf* Division also continued attempting to hold vital ground against strong Russian forces. Although the division never regained the strength it had possessed before the Battle of Kursk, it had received more replacements in men and equipment than most of the divisions. Part of its success in the southern sector of the front was down to the fact that it was stronger than most of the formations that fought around it. The *Totenkopf* contained three full battalions of *Panzergrenadiers*, one weak battalion of tanks with about half its normal establishment and more than half its normal artillery and flak. With this strength it managed to successfully halt the Soviet advance in mid-November. The division then dug in and prepared its units for another Russian assault. What followed was a battle that raged for almost three days, during which time *Totenkopf* destroyed a staggering 247 Russian tanks. However, *Totenkopf*'s success was short-lived.

On 25 November the Red Army once again attacked its positions, and for three days and nights the division endured one of the fiercest attacks in its history as an SS combat formation. In no less than ten days the Soviets once again renewed their offensive, smashed into the 384th Division and bulldozed past the left flank of the 1st Panzer Army. On 6 December the Russian flanks broke into open country and threatened Krivoy Rog from the north-west. As one of the crack 'fire brigade' divisions, the *Totenkopf* was ordered to be rushed to the crisis sector and once again displayed its skill and tenacity on the battlefield. While the SS troops held the Russian forces in check, on 19 December the 11th and 13th Panzer divisions were moved forward and launched a major counter-attack, with the *Totenkopf* leading the drive. The counter-attack once again restored the area from the clutches of the Red Army and the town of Krivoy Rog was in German hands. The desperate defence by the *Totenkopf* and its fellow divisions had bought enough time to remove the bulk of the supplies, ammunition, vehicles and rolling stock from the area that would have been irretrievably lost if the Russians had reached Krivoy Rog sooner.

Throughout January and February the winter did nothing to impede the Soviet offensives from grinding further west. Around the strategic town of Kirovograd Red Army units attacked, but soon found German resistance in the area stronger than expected. Some eleven German divisions, including the SS *Wiking* and the new Belgian Walloon volunteer unit SS *Sturmbrigade Wallonien*, which had recently been transferred from the Wehrmacht to SS control, were embroiled in an attempt to stem the Soviet push westwards. Here these strong German divisions held a salient into the Soviet lines between the towns of Korsun and Cherkassy. However, within days of tenaciously holding their positions, the Germans became cut off by General Nikolai Vatutin's 1st and General Ivan Konev's 2nd Ukrainian fronts. Trapped in the Korsun Pocket were some 50,000 men, a total of six German divisions, including the elite SS *Wiking* and the SS *Sturmbrigade Wallonien*. The trapped forces were designated *Gruppe Stemmerman* after their commander. The *Wiking* Division had some forty-three tanks and assault guns. Two assault gun battalions provided an additional twenty-seven assault guns. *Wiking* was the only armoured unit in the pocket, and with these tanks and assault guns they were ordered to drive the enemy back and perform an impossible feat by breaking out of the encirclement and destroying the enemy. Day and night the fighting raged, but the Russians, with some thirty-five divisions around the salient, inflicted terrible casualties. The constant pressure gradually saw the pocket shrink to some 40 square miles by early February.

As disaster loomed, a relief effort was quickly assembled. The *Leibstandarte* was hurried to the area. *Oberstleutnant* Franz Bake's Tiger tanks of the 503rd *Schwere Panzer-Abteilung* were ordered to help wrench open the pocket. However, the Tiger tanks and their supporting vehicles found the terrain in which they advanced very difficult. An unseasonal rise in temperature had caused a sudden thaw and turned the terrain into a boggy morass, making movement almost impossible in some areas. Nevertheless, deep in mud, the SS pushed forward, and by 8 February elements of the *Leibstandarte* and 16th Panzer Division had reached and established bridgeheads across the Gniloi Tickich River, west of Boyarka. *Gruppe Stemmerman* began immediately pulling back troops from north of the *Kassel* and attacking south to expand towards the relief forces on the north bank of the Gniloi Tickich.

By 13 February the spearheads of the division were within grasp of the encircled troops, but were exhausted by their efforts and ground to a halt on the line Lysanka-Oktyar-Chisinzy. While the *Leibstandarte* battled slowly forward, Hitler at last consented to the evacuation of the Korsun Pocket. On the night of 16 February, *Gruppe Stemmerman* received a communiqué from von Manstein ordering it to break out of the pocket at all costs.

Inside the pocket all the wounded had to be left behind, as did most of the artillery and heavy equipment. The SS *Sturmbrigade Wallonien* suffered terrible losses covering the rearguard, with almost three-quarters of its entire strength left dead on the battlefield. As the remnants pushed slowly forward nearer to the German lines, Russian fire intensified, inflicting even more casualties. In typical Waffen-SS style, the *Wiking* Division's only remaining tanks turned back and fought to the death, while the last of the brigade reached the German lines before being overrun. The SS *Das Reich* was another combat formation that had been rushed to help relieve the troops in the pocket. They were among the rearguard units, holding fast while the bulk of the encircled troops made good their escape. *Das Reich* had suffered heavy losses as a result of their self-sacrifice. Out of 5,000 soldiers that were sent to the area, some 1,121 of all ranks were killed in action.

In spite of the huge losses in men and equipment, some 33,000 German troops had escaped with their lives. Another major disaster had been averted in southern Russia. The distinguished performances of the Waffen-SS had once again further increased its reputation as the foremost fighting machine on the Eastern Front. The *Wiking* commander Herbert Otto Gille and *SS-Hauptsturmführer* Léon Degrelle, commander of the Walloons, were summoned to Hitler's East Prussian headquarters, *Wolfsschanze* ('The Wolf's Lair'), and decorated. Gille received the Oak Leaves and Swords, and Degrelle the Knight's Cross.

Following the break-out in the Korsun Pocket the *Das Reich* Division, now totally depleted with most of its armour lost in the battle, was withdrawn from the front and sent to France for a rest and refit. A *Kampfgruppe* from the *Das Reich* Division under the command of *SS-Oberführer* Heinz Lammerding remained in southern Russia to continue German attempts to try to hold back the Red Army.

During March 1944, Army Group south was forced to make a slow fighting withdrawal to the Dniester River on the border with Romania. On 11 March, parts of the *Totenkopf* Division that had been fighting fanatically as it pulled back towards the Dniester were air-lifted to Balta to form the core of a new defensive position there. As the Russians resumed their offensive towards the Dniester the *Das Reich Kampfgruppen*, shattered from weeks of intensive combat, continued doggedly to defend every foot of ground. All along the battered front lines there was no respite.

The Soviet offensive tore a massive hole between the 1st and 4th Panzer armies at Proskurov. Before the gap could be successfully sealed, the entire 1st Panzer Army found itself totally encircled in a huge pocket near the town of Kamenets-Podolsky. Among the units trapped were the *Das Reich Kampfgruppen* and the *Leibstandarte*. In the long fierce battle that ensued *Das Reich* recaptured the town of Isyaslavl and stemmed the Red Army drive. Fighting around the town raged until 14 March, until which time losses to the battered grenadier companies had become so severe that they could no longer hold their lines.

As the situation deteriorated further across the whole area, panic-stricken front-line commanders pleaded for the release of the last Waffen-SS reserves to restore the situation. At this point Hitler agreed and allowed at once for the II SS Panzer Corps, which consisted of the 9th SS Panzer Division *Hohenstaufen* and the 10th SS Panzer Division *Frundsberg* to be rushed to the Eastern Front from France. Both *Hohenstaufen* and *Frundsberg* had been trained for almost a year and equipped to a high standard and consisted mainly of *Reichdeutsche* Germans. The soldiers were regarded as crack SS troops, and the basis of the divisions had been built around a cadre of personnel from units such as the *Leibstandarte* and *Das Reich*.

Although regarded as second-rate SS divisions, these troops were formidable opponents, but despite their best efforts nothing could mask the fact that they were dwarfed by the superiority of the Red Army. During the second half of January the Russians had ploughed their way westwards, and by the end of the month had reached German fortified positions at the city of Narva. On the west bank of the Narva River SS units had constructed heavily-defended emplacements. Here the soldiers of *Nordland* and *Nederland* were determined to stand firm and fight in what became known as the Battle of the European SS.

The main brunt of the Soviet attack was to fall on Steiner's SS Corps, positioned east of Narva. On 3 February, the Soviet assault was finally unleashed and a bloody battle ensued. Almost immediately a Russian armoured group quickly penetrated the German line and established a bridgehead on the western bank of the Narva. The *Nordland*'s *Panzer-Abteilung*, named *Hermann von Salza*, commanded by *SS-Obersturmbannführer* Paul-Albert Kausch and assisted by Tiger ace *Leutnant* Otto Carius and a platoon of four Tigers, crashed into action. Quickly eliminating the Soviet armour, the Panzers and Tigers then began supporting the SS Grenadiers as they cleaned out the Soviet infantry. Although the crisis was temporarily averted in the centre, further north Red Army forces successfully established a bridgehead near the village of Siivertsi. To the south of the city of Narva, in the zone defended by an ad hoc army *Abteilung* named *Narwa*, Russian soldiers crossed the river and threatened to cut off Steiner's SS corps and two Wehrmacht units. The 502nd *Schwere-Panzer-Abteilung* was moved into the threatened area and quickly stabilized the German line. To strengthen the German defence, the newly-formed Estonian

20th *Waffengrenadier Division der SS* (*Estnische Nr. 1*) Division was rushed into the line and attached to Steiner's Corps. Steiner threw the division into battle on 20 February against the Siivertsi bridgehead. The Estonian SS soon proved themselves in combat, and within nine days of continuous fighting, Red Army troops had been pushed back across the river.

To the south, however, the German combat formations were collapsing under a fresh Soviet assault. By 24 February the Russian spearheads had reached the main rail line supplying the Narva area and threatened to encircle Steiner's Corps to the north. Despite heavy resistance the Red Army pushed forward, using heavy artillery and armour to smash through the German defences. *Armee-Abteilung Narwa* rushed forces south to halt the Soviet advance. A battalion from the *Nordland*'s *26.SS-Panzergrenadier* Regiment *Norge* was also brought south to help bolster the disintegrating line.

All along the German defensive line fierce fighting continued for weeks and months in Narva, with the Russians obtaining little ground against the tenacious efforts of both the Waffen-SS grenadiers and armoured units. In fact the defence of Narva was so tenacious that German units grimly held on to it until June.

By the summer of 1944 the Waffen-SS were fully aware that the Red Army had only been delayed, not halted. As both the southern and northern fronts withdrew and tried their best efforts to stabilize their precarious defences against a growing enemy force, news had reached them that the Allies had landed in Western Europe. Once again it was the Waffen-SS divisions that Hitler looked upon to save the desperate situation, but this would rob vital armoured units from a deteriorating Eastern Front.

In fact, during 1944 the *Panzerwaffe* were better supplied with equipment than during any other time on the Eastern Front thanks to the armaments industry. In total some 20,000 fighting vehicles including 8,328 medium and heavy tanks, 5,751 assault guns, 3,617 tank destroyers and 1,246 self-propelled artillery carriages of various types reached the Eastern Front. Included in these new arrivals were the second generation of tank destroyers, the Jagdpanzer IV, followed by the Hetzer and then the Jagdpanther and Jagdtiger. In fact, tank destroyers and assault guns would soon outnumber the tanks, which was confirmation of the *Panzerwaffe*'s obligation to perform a defensive role against overwhelming opposition. All these vehicles would have to be irrevocably stretched along a very thin Eastern Front, with many of them rarely reaching the proper operational level. Panzer divisions were also often broken up and split among hastily-constructed battle groups or *Kampfgruppen* drawn from a motley collection of armoured formations. Yet still these battle groups were put into the line operating well below strength. The demands that were put upon the *Panzerwaffe* during the spring and summer of 1944 were immeasurable. The constant employment, coupled with the nightmare of not having enough supplies, was a worry that perpetually festered in the minds of the commanders. The Red Army, encouraged by the Germans' dire situation, was now mounting bolder operations aimed directly against the German front.

With renewed confidence, Soviet commanders began drawing up plans for a massive concentration of forces along the entire front line in central Russia. The new summer offensive was to be called Operation BAGRATION and its objective was to annihilate Army Group Centre.

On the morning of 22 June, the third anniversary of the Soviet invasion, Operation BAGRATION was launched against Army Group Centre. The three German armies opposing them had 37 divisions, weakly supported by armour, against 166 divisions supported by 2,700 tanks and 1,300 assault guns. At the end of the first week of BAGRATION the three German armies had lost between them almost 200,000 men and 900 tanks; the 9th Army and 3rd Panzer Army were almost decimated. The remnants of the shattered armies trudged back west in order to try to rest and refit what was left of its Panzer units and build new defensive lines. Any plans to regain the initiative on the Eastern Front were doomed forever.

Seven photographs taken in sequence showing a Panther battalion struggling through mud on the Eastern Front in late 1943. By August 1943 the Waffen-SS Panzer divisions *Leibstandarte*, *Totenkopf* and *Wiking* all received a single company of the new modified Panther Ausf.D variant. In the same period, the 1st Battalion, SS Panzer Regiment *Das Reich* also received forty-nine improved Ausf.D Panthers to equip two of its tank companies, plus its regimental staff company. In late August, the battalion rejoined the *Das Reich* Division on the Russian front and began operating very successfully with a number of kills. One of the first Waffen-SS divisions to be re-equipped with an entire battalion of Panthers for operations on the Eastern Front was the 2nd SS Panzer Division *Das Reich*. However, by the end of 1943 *Das Reich* had lost all of its forty-nine Panthers while operating around the city of Zhitomir in the Ukraine. (*NARA*)

612

612

612

613

Taken in sequence here are two photographs showing Panther crew members during a rest. A typical Panther battalion was organized into a staff company comprising a communications platoon of various armoured reconnaissance and communication vehicles, engineer and anti-aircraft platoons. The Panzer Company comprised three or four tanks in each, consisting of medical service and repair vehicles. There was a workshop company comprising two workshop platoons consisting of a recovery platoon, communication, armourer and spare part detachment. This high degree of support was required not only to maintain the Panther in an effective offensive role but to keep it in fighting condition. *(NARA)*

Two *Totenkopf* Panther crew members rest during a respite in operations. One of the crew members appears to be writing a letter home to one of his loved ones. *(NARA)*

Three photographs showing Panther *Totenkopf* crewmen, two of them in the turret and the commander standing in the cupola. By the end of 1943, there were ever-increasing demands from the front line for Panthers, and it was the Waffen-SS Panzer divisions that were given priority. During the autumn of 1943 a large number of the Ausf.A variants began to enter service, and it was Hitler who decided over the next year that each Waffen-SS Panzer Division would receive entire battalions of Panther tanks to replace their existing under-gunned and under-armoured mid-range Pz.Kpfw.IIIs. Hitler was determined that the fortunes of the Eastern Front would be decided by utilizing the Panther and Tiger as the backbone of this success. *(NARA)*

An Sd.Kfz.10/4 hauling an Sd.Ah. 51 ammunition trailer for the mounted 2cm FlaK gun. This half-track belongs to a FlaK battalion of the SS Volunteer *Sturmbrigade Langemarck*, which comprised Waffen-SS Flemish recruits. This *Sturmbrigade* consisted of an anti-tank *Panzerjäger* company, an assault gun battalion equipped with StuGs and a FlaK battalion. In October 1943, the brigade was renamed 6th SS Volunteer *Sturmbrigade Langemarck*. In December 1943, the *Langemarck* was sent to the front. Another Flemish Waffen-SS division to see action was the 27th SS Volunteer Division *Langemarck*. It was sent to the Ukraine where it fought alongside *Das Reich* around Kiev and Zhitomir. In January 1944 the *Langemarck* and elements of *Das Reich* were encircled by Soviet forces near Zhitomir. Despite this, they fought their way out of the cauldron, suffering heavy casualties and losing the majority of their heavy equipment and vehicles. By early March, the brigade had been reduced to 400 men. At the end of April, the shattered *Langemarck* was ordered back to Bohemia for re-forming.

An SS crew member belonging to the *SS-Panzergrenadier Regiment 24 Danmark* smiles for the camera while the special maintenance team repairs an engine of what appears to be a Pz.Kpfw.III. Special tank maintenance companies, which kept the vehicles in fighting condition, were extensively used on the Eastern Front. Much was owed to the success of these tank battalions by their well-equipped maintenance teams. Out in the field they were able to quickly repair the combat damage and return vehicles to the battlefield to inflict more harm on the enemy.

(**Above**) Two Panthers halted in a field. By February 1944, the new improved Ausf.G variant was sent to the Eastern Front. They performed so well that the Waffen-SS were eager to receive these new models. The first elite division to be supplied with large numbers was the 5th SS Panzer Division *Wiking*. By the spring both the division's Panzer battalions were re-equipped entirely with a total of 160 Panthers, which was against the policy of allocating just one Panther battalion to each SS armoured division. Despite this, in contravention the *Wiking* Division became the most potent SS armoured formation on the Eastern Front and was used extensively to halt the Soviet drive westwards.

(**Opposite, above**) An Sd.Kfz.263 advances across a field. The long-range radio set was accommodated by the provision of both large frame and telescopic mast antennas.

(**Opposite, below**) *Wiking* troops clad in their SS winter anoraks grey side out are seen on the march here along a muddy road with the support of a half-track. (*NARA*)

A *Wespe* self-propelled gun is seen here during operation in the early spring of 1944. These vehicles served in the armoured artillery battalions of SS divisions. The *Leibstandarte* became the first SS division to field the *Wespe*. *Das Reich* and *Totenkopf* also received these vehicles in late 1942 and early 1943. By 1944 they were used extensively by the Waffen-SS. *(NARA)*

A battery of Hummels in a field. From the spring of 1943 a single battery of six Hummels plus one gun-less Hummel munitions carrier were allocated to Wehrmacht and Waffen-SS Panzer divisions. *(NARA)*

Four photographs depicting the StuG III Ausf.G. By 1944 the StuG III was used extensively on the Eastern Front and served with select SS assault gun battalions. It was by this period of the war that these assault guns, which fought bitter defensive actions, came into their own and revealed their true capabilities as tank killers. In fact, one such battalion, the 2nd Assault Gun Battalion *Das Reich*, between 5 July 1943 and 17 January 1944 claimed the destruction of some 129 Soviet tanks alone for a loss of just two StuG IIIs. (*NARA*)

A well-camouflaged Pz.Kpfw.IV Ausf.G of the 10th Panzer Division *Frundsberg* during operations in the Tarnopol area. The division was mainly formed from conscripts and it was at Tarnopol in April 1944 that it first saw action and later took part in the relief of German troops cut off in the Kamenets-Podolsky Pocket.

Chapter Five

Retreat: Defensive Battles in the East

With renewed confidence, Soviet commanders began drawing up plans for a massive concentration of forces along the entire front line in central Russia. The new summer offensive was to be called Operation BAGRATION and its objective was to annihilate Army Group Centre.

Over a period of several weeks the Russian offensive saw the complete collapse of Army Group Centre with divisions reeling back across a scarred and devastated battlefield to the borders of the Baltic States and into Poland. What was left of Army Group Centre was given to Field Marshal Walther Model, known as Hitler's 'fireman'. Model sent the *Totenkopf* Division to the city of Grodno, and there it was ordered to hold the right flank of the 4th Army in the north and the left wing of the 2nd Army in the south. Here in the city of Grodno this crack SS division held on to its crumbling positions, fighting off continuous attacks and bitter street-fighting that was reminiscent of some of the close-quarter battles that had raged at Stalingrad. However, outnumbered seven to one in troop strength and ten to one in tanks, the *Totenkopf* Division was gradually ground down in a battle of attrition and by 18 July requested permission to abandon their receding lines. Model agreed at once and ordered the withdrawal of the division west in the retreat towards the Polish capital of Warsaw.

During the last week of July the Russians pushed forward and rolled across the ravaged countryside of Poland through the shattered German front. On 24 July in the southern sector of the front, the 1st Panzer Army still held the town of Lwów and its front to the south. However, behind the Panzer army 50 miles west of Lwów massive Soviet forces were closing to the San River on the stretch between Jarosław and Przemyśl. Further north in the centre Model had feverishly regrouped his forces in an attempt to defend Siedlce, Warsaw and the Vistula south to Puławy. The *Totenkopf* Division was once again thrown into battle, this time along with the elite armoured Paratroop Division known as the *Hermann Göring Felddivisionen*. Both divisions were ordered to hold the city of Siedlce 50 miles east of Warsaw. For four days in the face of strong Russian armoured strikes both divisions held their lines at great cost, allowing the 2nd Army to retreat to the Vistula River. On 28 July, they abandoned Siedlce and continued a fighting withdrawal towards Warsaw.

Over the coming week fighting in the area was fierce, but both divisions fought to the bitter death, slowing the Russian onslaught and allowing Model to reorganize a defence along the river. As for the Soviet forces, having advanced another 200 miles in two weeks, they had temporarily outstripped their supplies. The offensive ground to a halt on the Vistula in early August. The brief lull in fighting helped Model to gradually gain strength and reorganize his defensive positions. The *Totenkopf* and *Wiking* divisions formed the 4th Panzer Corps commanded by *SS-Gruppenführer* Herbert Gille, and Model placed this corps 30 miles north-east of Warsaw where he expected the renewal of the Russian offensive.

Over the next few days north-west of the city tanks and grenadiers of the *Totenkopf* and *Wiking* divisions grimly held out, repulsing a number of vicious Russian attacks. The Red Army then regrouped and once again resumed their attack, which fell on the *Totenkopf*. For four days SS troops fought a gauntlet of heavy fighting. Russian air support hammered the German front lines day and night until the *Totenkopf* and the remainder of the Panzer Corps withdrew from its battered and blasted positions west towards Warsaw. By 10 September heavy fighting engulfed the suburbs of the city with *Totenkopf* successfully defending its positions. For ten days, until the Red Army offensive petered out, the SS managed to hold their lines in spite of the high losses. During the next few weeks until 10 October there followed a lull in the fighting until the Russians launched yet another offensive, which forced the 4th Panzer Corps to retreat 20 miles westwards.

By 27 October the front had once more been stabilized and the Red Army abandoned further assaults against the 4th Panzer Corps. Calm returned to the front around Warsaw and both Wehrmacht and Waffen-SS divisions tended to their wounded, re-equipped the best they could and dug another defensive line. The *Totenkopf*'s performance in these defensive battles had demonstrated the effectiveness of using the Waffen-SS armoured units as a special 'fire brigade' force. They had fought off many attacks against an enemy sometimes ten times their strength, and had provided Model's soldiers with a band of men that were able to be rushed from one danger zone to another and plug gaps in the front wherever they appeared.

Yet in spite of the dogged defence and the new arrival of Panzers rushed to the front including the delivery of the Tiger E and the King Tiger B tanks, which were undoubtedly formidable fighting machines, they did nothing to alleviate the overall predicament that was increasingly making itself felt along the entire battered and worn Eastern Front. With too few of them delivered, Tigers, Panthers, assault guns and tank destroyer crews found that they were too thinly stretched to make any considerable dent against the growing tank might of the Red Army. Many of the tanks and their crews were consequently lost. This led to a high volume of replacement crews that did not have sufficient time to be properly trained, and as a result losses soared even higher. Lack of fuel and spare parts, coupled with the need for trained crews, all played a major part in reducing the effectiveness of the German armour in the final year of the war.

During the last months of the year the situation on the Eastern Front further deteriorated. In the south Malinovsky's 2nd Ukrainian Front had broken through powerful German defences and the Red Army reached the Bulgarian border in early September. Within a week, Russian troops reached the Yugoslav frontier and on 8 September Bulgaria and Romania declared war on Germany. By 23 September, Soviet forces arrived on the Hungarian border and immediately raced through the country for the Danube, finally reaching the river to the south of Budapest. It was here in Hungary that Hitler placed the utmost importance on defending what he called the last bastion of defence in the east. Against all military logic, he felt that it was Hungary and not the Vistula River in Poland that presented a natural barrier against an advance on Germany. For this reason he drew off his premier Waffen-SS divisions, including *Totenkopf* and *Wiking* which were vitally required along the Vistula River, and transferred them to Hungary, once again depleting the Eastern Front of vital manpower and armour.

In Poland the whole military position was on the point of disintegration. For the German defenders it had been a gruelling battle of attrition. Fortunately for the surviving German forces, the Soviet offensive ran out of momentum by October. Their troops were too exhausted and their armoured vehicles were in great need of maintenance and repair. It seemed that the Germans were spared from being driven out of Poland, but only temporarily.

A whitewashed *Wespe* battery with their 10.5cm gun barrels elevated in preparation for a fire mission during winter operations in early 1944.

The commander of a Pz.Kpfw.III converses with another officer. Note that the rear plate of the *Schürzen* is missing.

A *Wespe* crew member wearing his winter whites waves to the photographer as he passes by. Note the interesting vertical grey wavy lines that break up the overall whitewashed winter scheme of this vehicle. Although these self-propelled guns were scoring sizable successes in Russia, by mid-1944 the Allied bombing campaign was causing severe problems, and shortages of fuel and spare parts were beginning to cripple armoured units on the Eastern Front. By the end of the war only a handful of *Wespe* machines were captured intact.

A group of photographs taken during early 1944 showing Waffen-SS troops collecting mines from a half-track and carrying them to be laid. This unit belongs to the 9th SS Panzer Division *Hohenstaufen* of Panzer Regiment 3. Marders and a StuG III can also be seen supporting the drive. Arriving in late March 1944 on the Eastern Front, the division was formed into the II SS Panzer Corps and was sent into the attack near the town of Tarnopol. In three days of combat, the *Hohenstaufen* destroyed seventy-four Soviet tanks, eighty-four self-propelled assault guns, twenty-one anti-tank guns and twelve mortars. *(NARA)*

The crew of a Pz.Kpfw.IV can be seen here 'tarping' their vehicle in order to help conceal it from enemy ground or aerial observation. The tank has been purposely parked next to a building for camouflage purposes.

A SS *Wiking* Pz.Kpfw.III crew halted in a field. One crew member can be seen taking a drink from his canteen.

Two photographs taken in sequence showing a modified Sd.Kfz.10 half-track mounting a 7.5cm PaK gun complete with splinter shield. The vehicle is being demonstrated to a group of Waffen-SS officers in the field. *(NARA)*

A StuG III on the advance. Despite the StuG's proven tank-killing potential and its service on the battlefield, the vehicle gradually deprived the infantry of the vital fire support for which the assault gun was originally built in order to supplement the massive losses in the Waffen-SS armoured arsenal.

A Panther belonging to the SS *Wiking* during operations in Kowel in 1944.

Four photographs showing Tiger tanks from an SS Panzer Company from the 19th Waffen Grenadier Division of the SS (2nd Latvian). Initially a Latvian brigade known as the Gross Brigade, it was formed in 1944 from the SS Training and Reserve regiments based in Dundaga, Latvia in order to keep the road to Riga open and to counter the Red Army's summer offensive, which had captured Mitau and Tukums and put the whole of Courland in danger. The SS Panzer Brigade was formed from the SS Panzer Training and Replacement Regiment based in Dundaga, Latvia and the SS Panzer Troop Training Regiment *Seelager* based at the training grounds at Ventspils together with the SS Reconnaissance Training Battalion formed the brigade. The brigade began forming on 8 August 1944 under the command of *Sturmbannführer* Martin Gross, and initially comprised two infantry battalions, a Panzer battalion of two companies with Pz.Kpfw.III and IV, a reconnaissance battalion, a StuG battalion, a pioneer company and a FlaK company. The brigade was dispatched to the front lines where it fought a series of counter-attacks towards Libau in Latvia. It was then reinforced on 15 August when a Tiger tank company was attached from the 103 SS Heavy Panzer Battalion and two batteries of artillery from the 19th Waffen Grenadier Division.

Two photographs taken in sequence showing a crew member belonging to the 19th Waffen-SS Division of the 103rd SS Heavy Panzer Battalion undertaking maintenance to a Tiger tank wheel. *(NARA)*

Three photographs showing a Tiger crew from 103 SS Heavy Panzer Battalion, attached to the Latvian 19th Waffen Grenadier Division, cleaning the 8.8cm KwK 36 gun tube of their vehicle during the summer of 1944. *(NARA)*

Three photographs showing the crew from 103 SS Heavy Panzer Battalion, attached to the Latvian 19th Waffen Grenadier Division, resupplying their Tiger with armour-piercing shells. *(NARA)*

Chapter Six

The End: Fighting for Survival

While IV SS Panzer Corps and two *Panzergrenadier* divisions were transferred to Army Group South to relieve Budapest, the *Panzerwaffe* continued to rigidly commit everything it still had. Despite the dogged resistance of many of the tank crews and supporting troops, there was no coherent strategy and any local counteroffensives were often blunted with severe losses. The Soviets possessed too many tanks, anti-tank guns and aircraft for the Panzers and they remained incapable of causing any serious losses or delay. Little in the way of reinforcements reached them, and those that were left holding a defensive position had already been forced into various ad hoc Panzer divisions that were simply thrown together with a handful of tanks and *Panzergrenadiers*. Many of these hastily-assembled formations were short-lived. The majority were either completely decimated in the fighting or had received such a mauling in battle that they were reorganized into a different ad hoc formation under a new commander.

For the armoured fighting units left on the Eastern Front, they fought on with shortages of every kind, which was affecting most of the old and experienced Panzer divisions. The Soviets had unmatchable matériel superiority, and yet, despite this major drawback, in late 1944 armoured vehicle production including tanks, assault guns and self-propelled assault guns was higher than in any month before May 1944. In October and November 1944 assembly plants managed to turn out 12,000 trucks by rebuilding disabled vehicles and transporting them to both the Eastern and Western fronts. Truck strengths, especially those authorized for Panzer and *Panzergrenadier* divisions, were already critically low. By the end of the year the problem had become so bad that it was proposed to mount the *Panzergrenadiers* on bicycles.

In a drastic attempt to sustain Germany's combat strength the Panzer brigades had two battalions and *Panzerjäger* brigades one battalion. However, despite these fervent efforts to increase their combat strength, Panzer units and individuals of Panzer and *Panzergrenadier* divisions were too exhausted to avert the situation decisively. As a result the Russians continued pushing forward while German forces retreated through Poland to East Prussia. Also along the Baltic coast Soviet forces advanced, crushing those German units which were all that remained of the once mighty Army Group North. Hitler refused to allow the evacuation of twenty divisions – 500,000 men – that had been bypassed in the Kurland peninsula. These heavy attacks eventually cut the vast territory formerly occupied by Germany in the north-east to a few small pockets of land surrounding three ports: Libau in Kurland, Pillau in East Prussia and Danzig at the mouth of the Vistula. Here along the Baltic German defenders were reorganized as Army Group Centre in East Prussia and Army Group Kurland, the former Army Group North. All the German forces were under strength, and their defensive capabilities depended greatly on the old Prussian and Silesian fortresses of Breslau, Stettin, Küstrin, Folburg, Insterburg and Königsberg.

Massive though the Soviet force was in the Baltic, it was nothing compared to the forces available to the Red Army further south. There the winter offensive was to be a massive two-pronged attack through the rest of Poland: one leading along the Warsaw-Berlin axis commanded by Zhukov, with the other for Breslau under the command of General Konev. On 12 January 1945, the Eastern Front erupted with a massive advance as Konev's offensive began with the 1st Ukrainian Front making deep wide-sweeping penetrations against hard-pressed German formations. The Russian offensive was delivered with a weight and fury never before experienced on the Eastern Front. On the first day of the offensive the 4th Panzer Army took the full brunt of an artillery barrage, followed by an armoured attack by the 1st Byelorussian Front. It had total numerical superiority over the Germans with 7 to 1 in armour alone. The vast tide of the Red Army soon swallowed up the battlefield and by the end of the first day of the new offensive it had torn a huge breach more than 20 miles wide in the Vistula Front. The 4th Panzer Army had almost ceased to exist. Krakow was immediately threatened and German forces quickly manoeuvred to defend this ancient city.

On 14 January, Zhukov's 1st Byelorussian Front began its long-awaited drive along the Warsaw-Berlin axis, striking out from the Vistula south of Warsaw. The city was quickly encircled and fell three days later. The frozen ground ensured rapid movement for the Russian tank crews, but in some areas these massive advances were halted for a time by the skilful dispositions of the *Panzerwaffe*. Determinedly they held out in small groups of grenadiers supported by Panzers, until they too were annihilated or forced to fall back. What forces were available to try to stem the Red Army's advance to the frontiers of the Reich were pulled together into a new army group, *Army Group Vistula*. This group was positioned behind the threatened front and consisted mainly of *Volkssturm* units and militia groups too young or old to serve in the regular army. Along this weak front, a number of volunteer SS units and ad hoc Panzer formations bolstered the under-strength and under-trained forces, but they too had little with which to impede the Russian onslaught.

Over the next few days nothing could prevent the Soviet advance. On 25 January the Russians stood in front of Breslau and two days later the city of Memel fell. As German forces continued to fall back, they tried frantically to prevent the Red Army from bursting across the borders of the Reich and onto the Oder, which was no more than 50 miles from the Reich capital of Berlin.

By early February 1945 German forces in the east had been driven back to the Oder, the last bastion of defence before Berlin. Only three weeks earlier, the Eastern Front was still deep in Poland. Now Upper Silesia was lost, in East Prussia German forces were smashed to pieces, West Prussia and Pomerania were being defended by depleted troops thrown together, and the defence of the Oder was now being entrusted to exhausted armies that had been fighting defensive actions for months in Poland along the Vistula. What was left of these forces were supposed to hold the Oder Front and fight to the death.

Along 200 miles of the defensive front the remaining Panzer divisions had no more than 70 tanks strung out along the front lines and were almost totally unprotected. On every 4 miles they had one Panzer, and on every 6 miles one battalion. They were confronted by an enemy force made up of three tank armies consisting of thousands of tanks. Against this massive Soviet force were the German 9th, 4th Panzer and 17th armies that fielded some 400,000 troops, 4,100 artillery pieces and 1,150 tanks. The First Byelorussian and First Ukrainian fronts had the Germans outnumbered on average by 10.1 in tanks and self-propelled artillery, and 9.1 in artillery and troops. On the First Byelorussian Front alone, this Russian army had more infantry, tanks and artillery than the entire German army on the Eastern Front.

Despite overwhelming Soviet superiority, German forces prepared their defensive positions along the Oder. On the night of 14 February the 11th SS Panzer Army, formed by SS *Reichsführer* Heinrich Himmler, actually mounted an attack, code-named Operation *SONNENWENDE*, and hit weak Russian units with its tanks. Although the daring Panzer attack caught the Russians by surprise, *SONNENWENDE* was no more than a reprieve for the Germans. Along whole areas of the front the once proud Panzer divisions had been reduced to skeletal formations on a stricken field. They were now not only vastly outnumbered but seriously lacked fuel supplies, lubricants and ammunition. When parts of the front caved in, armoured formations were often forced to destroy their equipment so that nothing was left for the conquering enemy. The Germans no longer had the manpower, war plant or transportation to accomplish a proper build-up of forces on the Oder. Commanders could do little to compensate for these deficiencies, and in many sectors of the front they did not have any coherent planning in the event that the defence of the river failed.

When the Russians successfully attacked the Oder in mid-April 1945, the hotchpotch force of what was left of both Wehrmacht and Waffen-SS armoured forces fought in desperation as the Soviet thrust carved its way across the river, capturing the town of Küstrin and heading towards the Nazi capital. A few days later the 11th *SS Panzergrenadier Division Nordland* was rushed to Berlin and the SS Brigade *Nederland* was sent out of the capital to help stem the Russian advance. Inside the ruined city, part of the 15th *Waffengrenadier-Division der SS* from Latvia was ordered to take up defensive positions together with the Belgian *Langemarck* and *Wallonien* divisions and the remaining volunteers of the French *Charlemagne* Division. All these Waffen-SS grenadiers, with what was left of their armour, were to take part in the last apocalyptic struggle to save the Reich capital from the clutches of the Red Army.

As the Russians poured through along the Berlin highway, III SS Panzer Corps were given the task of scraping together enough armoured vehicles to defend the line on the 3rd Panzer Army's flank along the Finow Canal. North of the canal stood the 4th SS *Polizei* Division, the 5th *Jäger* Division and the 25th *Panzergrenadier* Division. Standing to the east of Berlin was the LVI Panzer Corps. Although these German formations fought bitterly to defend the capital from the advancing Red Army, by 24 April the Russians systematically completed the great encirclement of steel and fire around Berlin. The Battle of Berlin was doomed, but even during the battle the commander of the 503rd Heavy Tank Battalion was able to report on 26 April that he still had six tanks ready for active service in the defence of the routes leading into Berlin. This was hardly enough tanks to stem the mighty Red Army, but even so courageous Tiger crews fought on ceaselessly, trying to prolong the death throes of the armoured units.

During the last days of the war most of the remaining Panzer divisions, which mainly comprised an assortment of under-strength battle groups, continued to fight as a unit until they were either destroyed or surrendered. Among the last Panzer divisions of the war formed, in name only, was Panzer Division *Clausewitz* which formed with two battalions of two tank companies each with a total of fifty-six tanks and assault guns. Although it saw extensive action, its success was limited and localized and did nothing to avert enemy operations.

(**Opposite**) Winter-clad grenadiers belonging to the *Wiking* Division are seen here hitching a lift on board a column of whitewashed StuG III Ausf.Gs. In order to maintain their speed in the field, accompanying infantry were often carried on the tanks and other armoured vehicles. When they ran into stiff opposition, they immediately dismounted to avoid taking heavy casualties.

A half-track with grenadiers wearing their distinctive Waffen-SS anoraks grey side out are seen here moving into action. They pass an MG 34 position with the gunner and feeder poised for a fire mission.

Four photographs taken in sequence showing a crew with their StuG III parking their vehicle inside a building in order to conceal it from both aerial and ground observation. By the latter part of the war the StuG was gradually called upon for both offensive and defensive fire support, where it was gradually embroiled in an anti-tank role trying to stem the might of the Red Army. During the last weeks of the war as fuel and spare parts became scarce, many StuGs were either destroyed or simply abandoned by their crews. *(NARA)*

A photo taken from on board the deck of a StuG III showing the commander inside his cupola as the vehicle advances along a snowy road. *(NARA)*

A column of StuGs belonging to a *Wiking* unit are seen here on a snowy road cautiously moving forward while two soldiers check the way ahead for land mines. *(NARA)*

Commanders from the 27th SS Volunteer Grenadier Division *Langemarck* converse in the field during Operation *SONNENWENDE* (SOLSTICE) in early 1945. The operation was to destroy a Soviet salient and to relieve the troops besieged in the town of Arnswalde. Within weeks the division would be attached to the III SS Panzer Corps, which was part of Felix Steiner's newly-formed IX SS Panzer Army located on the lower Oder near Stettin. (NARA)

A *Wespe* during winter operations. This self-propelled vehicle has received a white wash coating and, for additional camouflage protection, saplings have been applied over parts of the armour in order to break up its distinctive shape.

A very muddy motorcycle dispatch rider is seen here smiling with *Leibstandarte* commanders in the field during operations in Hungary.

A crew member is seen here on a road climbing into his Sd.Kfz.222 light armoured car belonging to the *Wiking* Division. *(NARA)*

An Sd.Kfz.251/10 mounting the 3.7cm PaK gun is seen here moving across a field. *(NARA)*

Waffen-SS soldiers wearing their distinctive summer camouflage smocks stand next to their tank. Note the spent shell cases piled on the ground. *(NARA)*

A column of Sd.Kfz.251s supported by a Pz.Kpfw.IV can be seen here advancing along a road that has been churned up by persistent heavy traffic.

Two young Hetzer crew members pose for the camera in front of their machine. The Hetzer entered production in the spring of 1944, and began joining the anti-tank battalions of SS grenadier divisions during the late summer of that year. Only four SS grenadier divisions received fourteen Hetzers. By 1 April 1945 only three SS divisions – the 10th *Frundsberg*, 20th SS Volunteer Grenadier Division Estonian and the 31st SS Volunteer Grenadier Division *Bohmen-Mahren* – received the Hezters. The last Waffen-SS division received the Hezter on 15 April: the 38th SS Grenadier Division *Nibelungen*.

Two crew members of a battle-worn Panther pose in front of their tank during the latter part of the war. On the Eastern Front, the few Panthers that were left in the field were thrown into ad hoc units for the final desperate efforts of defending the front lines. When the Russians finally attacked the Oder in mid-April 1945, there was still one complete Panther battalion left. The battalion went on to undertake successful defensive measures in spite of overwhelming opposition. However, within days the Russians carved their way across the Oder River, capturing the town of Küstrin and heading towards the Nazi capital.

Epilogue

By the spring of 1945, the bulk of the premier Waffen-SS divisions were carrying out a fighting withdrawal through Hungary and Austria, while on the receding Eastern Front those SS units still in action were principally European volunteer units. Even by this late stage of the war the level of determination and courage shown by both first- and second-rate SS combat formations was quite exceptional considering that many soldiers were totally aware there was no prospect of victory. However, in the closing days of the war most Waffen-SS soldiers were determined to withdraw west and surrender to the Anglo-American forces rather than to the Red Army. Few of them harboured any illusions as to the kind of treatment they would receive from the Russians. It was for this reason that the divisions of the once-vaunted SS decided to accept their fate in the west. The *Leibstandarte* surrendered to American forces at Steyr in Austria along with the remnants of *Hohenstaufen*. The *Totenkopf* capitulated to the Americans on 9 May after withdrawing its forces north-west of Vienna. However, their relief at escaping the Red Army was short-lived as the Americans soon handed over the *Totenkopf* to the Soviets, who had a score to settle with this particular division. Very few of the soldiers actually survived Russian captivity.

Remnants of *Das Reich* were in the area of Dresden frantically trying to defend the region from Russian forces swarming into the Reich. Some elements of the division capitulated to Russian forces, while another major grouping finished the war fighting against the American army in Austria, and a third group had been involved in a Prague rescue mission until they too surrendered to other US units in the border region of western Czechoslovakia.

While most of the remaining premier Waffen-SS divisions were captured, most of the foreign volunteers did not survive on the battlefields of Eastern Europe. The *Wiking* Division, with its predominantly western European troops, was annihilated while fighting outside Vienna. *Nordland* was decimated during the Battle of Berlin. The 14th *Waffengrenadier-Division der SS* surrendered in Czechoslovakia to Russian forces and most of the surviving elements were summarily executed. Part of the 15th *Waffengrenadier-Division der SS* was slaughtered in Berlin. *Horst Wessel* with its Hungarian volunteers surrendered to the Red Army near Prague. The 20th *Waffengrenadier-Division der SS* also capitulated near Prague, with many of the surviving soldiers being executed on the spot. The *Maria-Theresa* Division was destroyed in its homeland fighting for Budapest. The 25th and 26th *Waffengrenadier-Division* also fell into Russian hands in Hungary. *Nederland* was smashed to pieces during the last stages of the Battle of Berlin, and the remnants of the *Langemarck* and *Wallonien* divisions were also totally destroyed during the battle for the Reich capital, as were the volunteers of the French *Charlemagne* Division. The 30th *Waffengrenadier-Division* was also destroyed and its remnants were transferred to General Andrey Vlasov's Free Russian Army, but were soon in embroiled in heavy fighting and fell into Red Army hands.

Appendix I

SS Panzer Division Order of Battle

Division Headquarters

Commander of the division
General staff officer
Cartographical unit
Communications unit

Division escort
Military police
Quartermaster

Weapons Platoon

Mechanical
Captain Dr Physician

Captain Dr Dentist

Panzer Regiment

I Battalion
- 4 Companies (1–4)
- Workshop Company

II Battalion
- 5 Companies (5–9)
- Workshop Platoon

Anti-Tank Battalion

3 Companies of Assault Guns (1–3)

Panzergrenadier Regiment

I Battalion
- 4 Companies (1–4)

II Battalion
- 4 Companies (5–8)

III Battalion
- 4 Companies (9–12)
- Heavy Infantry Gun Company (13)
- Anti-Aircraft Company (14)
- Reconnaissance Company (15)
- Engineer Company (16)

Panzergrenadier Regiment

As above.

Armoured Reconnaissance Battalion

2 Panzer Scout Companies
2 Panzer Reconnaissance Companies

1 Heavy Company

Panzer Artillery Regiment

I Battalion
  3 Batteries
II Battalion
  3 Batteries
III Battalion
  4 Batteries

Rocket-Launcher Battalion

4 Batteries (1-4)

Anti-Aircraft Battalion

5 Batteries (1-5)

Armoured Engineer Battalion

1 (Armoured) Company (on IFV)
Engineer Companies, Bridge Convoy B

Armoured Signals Battalion

4 Communications Companies
1 Radio Company

Divisional Supply Troops

6 Vehicle Companies
1 Supply Company

Panzer Maintenance Battalion

3 Workshop Companies
1 (Weapon) Workshop Company
1 Spare and Repair Part Company

Provisioning Battalion

Bakery Company
Butcher Company
Divisional Food Services Office
Military Post Office

Medical Battalion

2 Medical Companies
1 Ambulance Company
1 Medical Supply Company

Replacement Battalion

Appendix II

Heavy Tank Battalion Order of Battle

A typical organization structure of a German Heavy Panzer Battalion in 1943:

Staff Company (3 tanks)

Communications Platoon
Engineer Platoon
Anti-Aircraft Platoon

1st–3rd Panzer Company (14 tanks each)

Company Detachment (2 tanks)
1st–3rd Panzer Platoon (4 tanks each)
Vehicle Repair Detachment
Combat Train I
Combat Train II
Baggage Train

Workshop Company

1st and 2nd Workshop Platoon
Recovery Platoon
Armour Detachment
Communications Detachment
Spare Parts Detachment

Heavy Units attached to the Waffen-SS

101st SS Heavy Panzer Battalion renamed in 1944 as SS Heavy Panzer Battalion 501 (*Schwere-SS-Panzerabteilung* 501), part of I SS Panzer Corps

102nd SS Heavy Panzer Battalion renamed in 1944 as SS Heavy Panzer Battalion 502 (*Schwere-SS-Panzerabteilung* 502), part of II SS Panzer Corps

103rd SS Heavy Panzer Battalion renamed in 1944 as SS Heavy Panzer Battalion 503 (*Schwere-SS-Panzerabteilung* 503), part of III (Germanic) SS Panzer Corps

104th SS Heavy Panzer Battalion (*Schwere-SS-Panzerabteilung* 104) was planned on 22 October 1943 for IV SS Panzer Corps, but was never formed.

Appendix III

Waffen-SS Armour

The bulk of the weapons and equipment used by the Waffen-SS throughout the war was more or less identical to that used by the Wehrmacht. A number of small arms, particularly those of foreign origin, saw considerable use in the units of the Waffen-SS due to the Wehrmacht's reluctance to supply sufficient quantities of German-produced hardware to Himmler's elite force. The Waffen-SS used a huge variety of weaponry, everything from small arms to heavy tanks. The elite SS Panzer divisions especially were equipped with Germany's best tanks and supporting armoured vehicles. From 1943 onwards, Waffen-SS troops were normally the first to be furnished with a host of new modern weaponry. However, even these elite troops were curtailed by never-ending shortages and were supplied with various weapons and equipment in order to sustain them on the battlefield long enough to drive back the growing enemy forces.

During the last two years of war the Waffen-SS supplemented the finest hardware the armaments industry could produce with standard popular weapons and equipment used by their Wehrmacht counterparts. Below are the principal types of weaponry used by the Waffen-SS, especially during operations on the Eastern Front.

Armoured Cars

Sd.Kfz.221, Sd.Kfz.222, Sd.Kfz.223, Sd.Kfz.231, Sd.Kfz.234, Sd.Kfz.260, Sd.Kfz.261, Sd.Kfz.263

Artillery Prime Mover Half-Tracks

Sd.Kfz.2, Sd.Kfz.6, Sd.Kfz.7, Sd.Kfz.8, Sd.Kfz.9, Sd.Kfz.10, Sd.Kfz.11

Light Armoured Reconnaissance Half-Tracks

Sd.Kfz.250 Series (12 variants)

Light Ammunition Carrier Half-Track

Sd.Kfz.252, Sd.Kfz.253

Medium Armoured Personnel Carrier Half-Track

Sd.Kfz.251 (22 variants)

Panzers

Pz.Kpfw.I, Pz.Kpfw.II, Pz.Kpfw.III (later variants), Pz.Kpfw.IV (later variants), Pz.Kpfw.V Panther, Pz.Kpfw.VI. Tiger I, Pz.Kpfw.VI. Tiger II

Assault Guns and Tank Destroyers

Sturmgeschütz (StuG III) (later variants)
Sturmgeschütz (StuG IV)
Panzerjäger Marder I, *Panzerjäger* Marder II, *Panzerjäger* Marder III, *Panzerjäger* Nashorn, *Panzerjäger* Hummel, *Panzerjäger Wespe*
Jagdpanzer IV/70 Tank Destroyer, *Jagdpanzer* 38(t) Hetzer, *Jagdpanzer* V *Jagdpanther*